SIGHT

The Art of Active Seeing

UNSEEN

John Schaefer

GoodYearBooks

An Imprint of ScottForesman
A Division of HarperCollinsPublishers

To Cathy, Emily, Chloe
and
Zena, Who Sees All

ACKNOWLEDGMENTS

I am indebted to the people of the Children's Photographic Workshop: Brent Herridge, Bruce Hucko, Rosalind Newmark, Jay Sharp, Tim Gangwer, Jean Antoine Badin, and Chad Johnson. Also Fred Wright, who has been a major artistic influence as well.

Special thanks to my friends and colleagues who helped with this book: Dr. Richard Schaefer, Carly Jimenez, Joan Goldsmith, Frank Anthony Smith, Randy Volheim, Allison Goodman, Ken Cloke, and Bob Immitt.

Credit for the actual production and editing is shared by Cathy Schaefer, Meg Moss, Karen Kohn, and Bobbie Dempsey, who gave birth to more than this book during the process.

To all the teachers and children I've had the honor to learn with, keep up the good work.

Finally, the vision and guidance of Tom Nieman made this book possible.

John Schaefer
June 1994

Goodyear Books
are available for most basic curriculum subjects plus many enrichment areas. For more GoodYearBooks, contact your local bookseller or educational dealer. For a complete catalog with information about other GoodYearBooks, please write:

GoodYearBooks
ScottForesman
1900 East Lake Avenue
Glenview, IL 60025

ON THE COVER: *FRED WRIGHT AND SUIT*

PREFACE

THE **ABILITY** TO UNDERSTAND (READ) AND

CREATE (WRITE) VISUAL **IMAGES**

This book is about paying attention, being aware. Our senses provide us with information. We process this information in an effort to make sense of the world and of our lives. The purpose of *Sight Unseen* is to help you and your children or students develop information processing skills and critical thinking skills—to help you become aware of your senses and use them well.

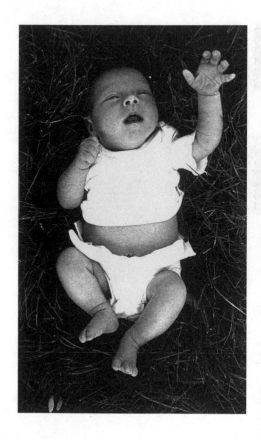

The book primarily emphasizes visual input; however, all the senses come into play. (Someone without sight might actually "see" better than a sighted person by relying upon their other senses and using them to their fullest.) By concerning ourselves with visual input, we will be dealing with everything from a beautiful sunset to the movie *Terminator 2*. Making good visual choices is a skill that empowers.

ACTIVE SEEING

ACTIVELY **AWARE** OF THE INFORMATION PROVIDED BY YOUR SENSE OF **SIGHT**. INHERENT

IN THIS **PROCESS** IS THE DEVELOPMENT OF **CRITICAL** INTERPRETATION **SKILLS**,

LEARNING TO MAKE SOMETHING OF WHAT YOU SEE. DO NOT CONFUSE **ACTIVE** SEEING

WITH TRYING TO SEE SOMETHING AT A DISTANCE. INCIDENTALLY, YOUR SENSES ARE

DESIGNED TO WORK BEST WHEN THEY ARE **RELAXED**, NOT STRAINING.

Much of our existence—who we are, what we believe, how we think and act—is based upon the input we receive through our sense of sight. As Michael Long wrote in his article, "The Sense of Sight":

As much as a third of the highest level of our brain, the cerebral cortex, is devoted to visual processing. Our eyes funnel two million fibers into our optic nerves, while the auditory nerve, the conduit for hearing, carries a mere 30,000 fibers. Sight mediates and validates the other senses; when we hear, smell, or touch something, we usually turn to see it also. (*National Geographic*, November 1992)

Unfortunately, a lack of visual, perceptual skills affects us just as much as a mastery of those skills. A person becomes confident through the acquisition of visual literacy skills, and one who lacks these skills is likely to be assigned the role of victim in our society.

Visual *literacy* has nothing to do with visual *acuity*. Whether you have 20/20 vision (meaning you can see what you should be able to see at twenty feet); or whether you have 20/200 vision (you can only see at twenty feet or closer what you should be able to see at two hundred feet), does not concern us here. Rather, the purpose of this book is to show you how to increase your level of awareness and become an *active* seer.

The commentary and activities in this book will help you understand the crucial role visual perception plays in the life of a citizen at the edge of the twenty-first century. Moreover, it will enable you to develop active seeing skills and teach those skills to others.

Sight Unseen is the product of years of personal experience with children in and out of the classroom, as well as at home. I have had the opportunity to work with hundreds of teachers, learning from them and their students, while also pursuing a career as a working photographer. Everything contained here has been proven to work with children, but certainly everything that works is not contained here. You will find *the basics* here. This is not meant to demean the material; rather, it is a foundation, a basis. The book is designed to empower and hopefully stimulate you to take it all to another level.

HOW *SIGHT UNSEEN* WORKS ←———————————————

Actually, the book doesn't work; you do. Seeing will be treated as work, an activity. There is nothing negative about work; it is simply "the utilization of energy." In fact, utilizing energy is often quite fun. (I'm sure that you can think of some examples!) This book is intended to make you work, but the work is designed to be enjoyable, because that is the way human beings learn most efficiently.

Even if you are a teacher, your knowledge of visual literacy may be limited, if, indeed, you have any at all. *Sight Unseen* will lead you through a series of activities devised to enable you to teach visual literacy, and the first person you teach will be yourself. You will not only learn; you will experience the conscious act of learning.

This will greatly benefit your students or children when you take on the role of teacher. Be forewarned, however: you will soon learn that when it comes to sense perceptions, the child is usually far superior to the adult. This leads to a healthy atmosphere of exchange, communication, and respect between adult and child. Teacher and child share in the same pleasurable experience—learning— thereby changing who they are for the better.

NOTE

THIS BOOK USES A COMMON TOOL OF **VISUAL** REPRESENTATION, THE **PHOTOGRAPH**, AS THE **PRIMARY** MEANS OF TEACHING **VISUAL LITERACY**. OTHER MEDIA SUCH AS **DRAWING** AND **VIDEO** WILL ALSO BE USED. THE LESSONS IN SIGHT UNSEEN APPLY TO ALL **TWO-DIMENSIONAL IMAGERY**—DRAWING, GRAPHIC **DESIGN**, AND EVEN **CAVE** PAINTING.

As you work with this book, keep these things in mind:

1. Although *Sight Unseen* focuses on seeing, that focus should not be at the expense of the other four valuable receptors: the senses of smell, hearing, taste, and touch. The book's exercises often overlap various sensory experiences. Since we learn by using a mixture of all of our senses, to attempt to limit learning to seeing would lack basic integrity.

2. You will need to be flexible; as you will see, this is a prerequisite for the development of superior visual literacy skills.

3. Every activity in this book can be easily expanded. Feel free to improvise. If you are a classroom teacher laden with lesson plans, take heart. You can adapt almost any activity to meet particular lesson plan objectives. If you can't come up with a way, ask your students—they will.

Some activities invite you and the children to discuss. This is an opportunity for all of you to create a written description of an image. Kids love relevancy (don't we all?), and imagery can be a powerful relevancy tool for language skills development. Play with it.

For example, a teacher's lesson plan might call for a social studies unit on immigration in present-day America. The images of almost any activity can be made

ANASAZI RUINS, UTAH

to communicate the effects of multiculturalism in a
community. Write about what the images represent.
How do they affect us? What do they mean to each of us?

Sight Unseen is essentially linear, each chapter
building on the previous one in a step-by-step learning
process. The Introduction provides instruction for teaching
visual literacy effectively. It contains proven tips that will
boost your confidence in your role as a child's learning
guide. You will experience the joy of learning and seeing
together as you work through the subsequent chapters.

Chapters 1 and **2** help you understand your eyes and how they work, explaining how to use them in a more effective manner to gain more from the world around you.

Chapters 3, 4, 5, and **6** discuss photography and how to use your new understanding of active seeing to create effective visual images, with or without a camera.

Chapters 7 and **8** investigate more advanced topics in composing, organizing, and framing images.

Chapters 9 and **10** explore the relationship between visual literacy and those denizens of our technological age— television and computers.

Chapter 11 is a guide to developing portfolios, or what I call Records of Achievement, the hard products that reflect what has been learned. Concrete results are an integral part of the learning process, whether you are working in a school system that requires portfolios, or you are teaching your own child. (In which case the future requires that you keep a record!)

Chapter 12 recommends a variety of experiences designed to further your own visual literacy.

Five levels of information run concurrently through-out the book. Each of the levels can be easily identified by its format:

1. **Text:** Basic explanatory text (unboxed)

2. **Activities:** Hands-on activities for the parent or teacher and child to do together to learn the material presented in the text. For those of you who do not like to sing along, you can learn quite a bit by simply reading the activities.

3. **Anecdotal Information:** "Real-life" experiences that complement the text and activities (shown in italic)

4. **Images:** Visual illustrations or communications, usually photographs, drawings, or graphs

5. **Key Phrases:** Quotes and sayings designed to stimulate various understandings (boxed)

SIGHT UNSEEN

TEXT →

THE PHOTOGRAPH

A photograph is a drawing on paper (graph) made with light (photo): a light-drawing (not a heavy drawing—although they can clearly communicate "heavy" concepts). Thus, a photograph is a drawing that is made using light. Sometimes we make drawings using pencils, crayons, or paint. In a photograph, we use the energy of the light to make the drawing.

WHAT'S IN A WORD?

WHY DO YOU THINK

KEY PHRASE

THE **LEAD** IN **PENCILS**

IS CALLED **GRAPHITE**?

RESPONSIBILITY

One morning I was passing out cameras to a fourth-grade class. I wanted them to handle the cameras with care, so I asked them to tell me what the word responsibility meant. Much to my surprise (and delight) hands immediately shot up, and one student shouted, "It means the ability to respond."

ANECDOTE

Of course this teacher, and her students, were way ahead of me. She had taught them that the best way to understand words is to break them up into any component parts and then guess at the meaning of these parts. Responsibility—"the ability to respond." I never heard it put so well. Now that's word power!

40

ACTIVITY 1.2: PERIPHERAL VISION

1. Ask the child to extend her arms, with straight elbows, to the side, parallel to the floor, and as far behind her back as possible. The child should extend the index finger on each hand pointing up perpendicular to the floor.

2. Ask her to stare straight ahead.

3. Now have the child, still staring only straight ahead, move her arms slowly forward, stopping when she can see her fingers with her peripheral vision. Through this exercise, she will notice the width of her peripheral vision and the narrowness of her focused vision.

4. Having established the outside limits of her peripheral vision, ask the child to repeat step 3, except

this time she should close her eyes while moving her arms forward a few inches, then open them to see if she can see her stationary fingers. Repeat until she sees her static fingers in her peripheral vision. She should notice that this time her angle of peripheral vision is narrower than before when she was trying to see her moving fingers. Why? The answer is in the next activity.

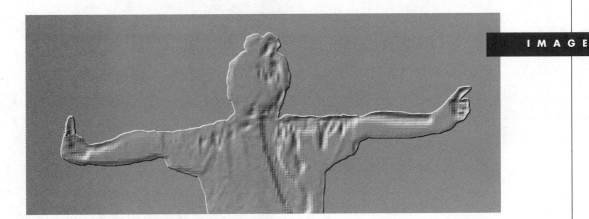

ASPECTS OF SEEING 15

A FINAL WORD

A final word about *truths*. All the "truths" in this book are subject to revision, by you, your students, and the scientific and educational communities—whoever discovers a different approach that works better. We are all pioneers on this journey of human learning. Remember, at one time Christopher Columbus was unquestionably a hero, and smoking cigarettes was the thing to do.

CONTENTS

CONTENTS

INTRODUCTION

LEADING A HORSE TO WATER

THE **PRESSURE** IS OFF—YOU CAN'T **TEACH** ANYONE ANYTHING.

YOU CAN ONLY **PROVIDE** SOMEONE WITH THE **OPPORTUNITY** TO LEARN.

CACTUS, CAPITAL REEF NATIONAL PARK, UTAH

IF ANY **LEARNING**, MEANING REAL CHANGING, IS TO OCCUR, IT IS THE RESPONSIBILITY

OF THE **INDIVIDUAL**, NOT THE TEACHER. IN **EDUCATIONAL JARGON**

IT'S KNOWN AS THE "**LEAD THE HORSE TO WATER**" MAXIM.

TEACHING AND LEARNING VISUAL LITERACY

For more than fifteen years I have had the pleasure of working in classrooms throughout the world with some of the finest teachers and students imaginable. I am confident that the material presented here is sound, perhaps because the ideas are not totally mine, but even more so because I have seen them work on real kids, in the real world. I have witnessed the lives of children (and adults) change, sometimes dramatically.

THE NAVAJO EXPERIENCE

In 1980 photographer/educator Bruce Hucko and I had the opportunity to work as Artists-In-Residence (a National Endowment for the Arts program) at an elementary school on the Navajo Indian reservation in Montezuma Creek, Utah. Many of the children there were graduating from sixth grade with English reading and writing skills comparable to those of first or second graders.

We used instant cameras since the nearest film developer was literally hundreds of miles away. The first photographs that they made taught us that if anyone in the classroom was short on intelligence it was us, for even entertaining the thought that these kids might be dumb or inferior. The photos were fabulous. Of course, the kids' English language skills were poor simply because they were speaking Navajo at home. Also, interestingly enough, Navajo is not a *written language. (English-speaking scientists have had their own need to create a written Navajo language, but it is certainly not in common use.) We began to realize as we looked at the children's well-composed, articulate photographs, that "what we had here was a failure to communicate," in this case a language problem.*

We had the children take turns doing the following exercise. A child would stand in front of the room and describe her photograph in English to the rest of the class who had not yet seen it. The kids in the class were armed with pencils and paper and were to draw the photograph she described. The object was to communicate effectively so that the photograph and drawings looked approximately the same. Invariably, the first attempt went something like this: The Navajo child shyly stands in the front of the room saying nothing, wanting no part of this activity. Hucko and I are burdened with guilt. Finally the child realizes that we may be crazy enough to leave her up there forever, so she blurts out a one-word description of her photo: "Playground." The rest of the kids start drawing like mad— they feel as though they've been waiting forever. They make all kinds of beautiful drawings of the playground. Unfortunately none is even close to the girl's photo, which is a very nice one of two girls swinging from the monkey bars. It is obvious to all that she did not communicate—translate her photograph into words—very well.

NAVAJO RESERVATION, UTAH

The next day she tries again with a different photograph. She speaks right up and is very specific about her image: "In the upper right-hand corner there is a triangle shape formed by…" and so on. This time all of the drawings bear an obvious resemblance to her photograph.

Hucko audiotaped her second description and transcribed it that night back in his hogan. (He enjoys living close to the earth.) The next morning he made mimeographed copies of her words. We gave this written description to another class and asked them to draw what was described. These drawings clearly matched her photo.

This activity brought the work full circle into a realization for the children, and for us: The exercise showed that the real world (the playground) could be communicated two-dimensionally on paper (the photograph). This two-dimensional representation (the photograph) could then be translated into English words and written in English symbols. The kids began to understand that these shapes, the English alphabet, could actually be used to represent something in their real world.

Reality ⟶ Photograph ⟶ Written English

This connection had profound repercussions. The kids' reading and writing skills increased dramatically (three years later the school received a Rockefeller Grant in recognition of educational excellence), Hucko never left the reservation, and I'm writing this book.

You, too, can experience these moments of wonder in teaching children. Before you tackle learning about and teaching visual literacy, though, you should think about the following ideas.

LANGUAGE ARTS/COMMUNICATION ←

Communication is the key word. Most of this book could probably be categorized as language arts directly linked to critical thinking skills. This relates to every other discipline, since they are all of necessity language-based in one form or another. Even mathematics is a language, a representation of reality (4+1=a basketball team). Whether you are a parent or a classroom teacher, you should have no trouble "justifying" the use of this book. The child you work with will be a better learner and a better communicator.

TEACHER/LEARNER

When I go into a classroom I always ask the kids: "Why do you think I'm here?" The answers range from "You're here to help us," to "For the money."

I respond: "I don't even know you kids, and I'm not sure I even like you. Why would I get out of bed to help you?!" and "I'm losing money by being here with you." Anyone in the field of education knows that you don't get into it for the money.

After a while the class realizes that I must be there for selfish reasons, and someone usually guesses: "Are you here to learn from us?" Exactly.

PREJUDICE: A DETERRENT TO LEARNING, A TOOL FOR TEACHING

Think about the word *prejudice*. It breaks down into two parts: *pre* and *judge*. This word has no positive connotations, except in the field of teaching and learning, where, when broken, prejudice can be a powerful tool. When someone's preconceived idea is shattered, their mind is opened; learning—change—can take place.

For example, if a student is wandering in the school halls at the inappropriate time and a teacher happens upon her, the student, instead of concocting a story, should simply tell the truth: "I shouldn't be in the halls now, I belong in my classroom. This is terrible behavior on my part." The shock value, playing against the teacher's preconceived idea (prejudice) of what the student will answer, will usually get the student off scot-free, ONCE.

The breakdown of prejudice is probably the only time that it can be seen in a positive light. For our purposes here, you must learn to recognize your prejudices and leave them behind, and you must help your students or child do the same.

PHOTOGRAPHER/EDUCATOR BRUCE HUCKO, NAVAJO RESERVATION

A TEACHABLE MOMENT

PRECONCEIVED **NOTIONS** **(PREJUDICES)** ARE THE ENEMY OF USING THE **SENSES** FOR ACCURATE **INFORMATION** GATHERING. HOWEVER, WHEN YOU BREAK OR **UNDERMINE** SOMEONE'S **PRECONCEIVED** IDEAS, HER **MIND** IS OPENED, FOR THE MOMENT. THIS IS A **TEACHABLE** MOMENT—AN OPPORTUNITY TO **CHANGE** THE PERSON, TO **EDUCATE** HER.

GUESSING FOR A LIVING

Be aware that you don't have all the answers, nor should you be expected to. Human beings learn by making mistakes. Take the pressure off yourself; if you don't know an answer, make a guess. If you're wrong, you'll learn. In taking this approach to learning, you'll have more fun, but even more importantly, you and the child will learn more efficiently.

LIGHT—THE AMBIGUOUS CONSTANT

SCIENTISTS **WORKING** AT THE HIGHEST LEVELS OF **KNOWLEDGE** GENERALLY AGREE FOR THE MOMENT THAT THE ONLY **CONSTANT** IN OUR WORLD IS THE **SPEED OF LIGHT** (186,000 MILES PER SECOND). YET THEY DON'T KNOW IF LIGHT IS A PARTICLE OR A **WAVE**; THEY CAN PROVE THAT IT **ACTS LIKE BOTH**! SO, IF THE TOP SCIENTISTS (SEEKERS OF KNOWLEDGE) ARE NOT SURE ABOUT THE **NATURE** OF THE ONLY CONSTANT IN THE **UNIVERSE**, WHAT ARE YOU WORRYING ABOUT?

GUESSING FOR A LIVING

I had introduced myself one morning to a fourth-grade class saying that I did a number of things and was not sure how to label my occupation. After about an hour I was about to launch into critiquing some designs the children had made. I assured them that my views were my own, and that I have had a history of being wrong (doesn't everyone?). At this point a young girl raised her hand and said, "I know what you do, you guess for a living!"

LEARNING FROM MISTAKES

A human being learns from her mistakes, as long as they are her own mistakes. If someone, a well-meaning teacher perhaps, puts a child in a situation in which she will fail, then the child will take no ownership or responsibility for her actions. The mistake will not be the child's, but the teacher's. It is critical that you, the teacher, be there for the child, holding her hand, giving her the security to accept the risks inherent in learning.

WHEELS FOR FEET

A few years ago I had the chance to babysit a four-year-old whom I hardly knew. I decided to take her roller-skating—to teach her something new so that she would remember me. We went to the local rink, and, much to her surprise, I strapped wheels to her feet and proceeded to take her out on an extremely slippery surface.

I held her up for a few minutes. She was very tense and nervous, and when I did let go of her, she came crashing down, hard, screaming and crying. Each time it was the same scenario. I was now certain that she would remember me. At the same time I began worrying about the exact phrasing of the local child abuse laws.

I carried her off the rink and bought her some popcorn. When the sobbing subsided we sat together and watched other kids, some her age, enjoying skating. I (not we) decided to try again. This time I promised not to let go of her. We skated around for a while, and then the most amazing thing happened—she let go of my hand. She fell, hard, again; but, amazing thing number two, she did not cry. From then on I continued to hold her hand until she let go. She still fell each time, but she did not cry and actually started to take a few steps on her own. Within twenty minutes she was "skating" around the rink—occasionally falling, wincing, but never crying.

Human beings learn by their mistakes. Our first efforts were a dismal failure because the falling was not her mistake, it was mine. I initiated it, I let go of her, she learned nothing (except maybe to hate me). Later she was driven to learn by her own will, and when she released my hand, skating became her responsibility. She owned the consequences, processing the information about skating and falling that she was learning. The act of learning was so powerful that it overrode the physical pain she was experiencing.

TAKE/MAKE WHAT YOU CAN

SOME OF THE **CONCEPTS** IN THIS BOOK WILL SEEM QUITE **BASIC** TO YOU. (THEY ARE MEANT TO BE—GOOD BASICS ARE **CRUCIAL**.) THEY MAY EVEN BE "**UNDER YOUR HEAD**." OTHERS MAY SEEM TOO **COMPLEX** OR DIFFICULT. IT IS **IMPORTANT** TO **KEEP** IN MIND THAT THIS BOOK IS **BASED** UPON A **WORKSHOP-TYPE** LEARNING EXPERIENCE THAT HAS **BENEFITED** THOUSANDS, FROM YOUNG **CHILDREN** AND EXPERIENCED **TEACHERS** TO **SENIOR** CITIZENS.

MAKE YOUR **EXPERIENCE ENJOYABLE**; TAKE/MAKE WHAT YOU CAN FROM THE **TEXT**, LOOK AT THE **PICTURES**, AND DO THE **ACTIVITIES**. THEY ARE DESIGNED TO CHANGE **FOREVER** THE WAY YOU **SEE** AND **UNDERSTAND** THINGS.

Yellowstone Fires, 1989

DEVELOPING VISUAL APPRECIATION SKILLS

Visual appreciation is based largely upon personal taste. A very good reason to design something a certain way is that it looks or feels good to you. This is not meant to discount the rules of good visual communication that you will work with in this book. Rather, it is meant to emphasize that paying attention to what you like will help you develop strong visual appreciation skills. Take some risks and trust your innate design abilities and those of the child.

ON WITH THE SHOW (AND TELL)

These are the basic concepts behind learning about and teaching visual literacy. Now let's look at the basics of visual literacy, starting with vision.

1 ASPECTS OF SEEING

BAT SIGHT

DAD, DID YOU **KNOW** THAT BATS **SEE** WITH THEIR **EARS**?!

Chloe, four years old

Barcelona, 1990

THE TECHNICAL SIDE OF SEEING

It is interesting to explore the way that our eyes, and subsequently our brains, process visual information. We actually see only a small point in the center of our visual frame in sharp focus. This is called the *point of centricity*. Everything else in our visual field is blurry, it is outside, or on the *periphery*, of the sharply focused central point. This is called *peripheral vision*.

ACTIVITY 1.1: POINT OF CENTRICITY

1. Hold up a pencil across the room from the child. Ask her to focus sharply on the point of the pencil.

2. Now ask the child to focus on the eraser. She should notice that even from across the room her eyes cannot see the entire pencil in focus at exactly the same time. In fact, if she becomes aware of her body, she will notice that in order to focus, her eye must move from the point to the eraser.

ACTIVITY 1.2: PERIPHERAL VISION

1. Ask the child to extend her arms, with straight elbows, to the side, parallel to the floor, and as far behind her back as possible. The child should extend the index finger on each hand pointing up perpendicular to the floor.

2. Ask her to stare straight ahead.

3. Now have the child, still staring only straight ahead, move her arms slowly forward, stopping when she can see her fingers with her peripheral vision. Through this exercise, she will notice the width of her peripheral vision and the narrowness of her focused vision.

4. Having established the outside limits of her peripheral vision, ask the child to repeat step 3, except this time she should close her eyes while moving her arms forward a few inches, then open them to see if she can see her stationary fingers. Repeat until she sees her static fingers in her peripheral vision. She should notice that this time her angle of peripheral vision is narrower than before when she was trying to see her moving fingers. Why? The answer is in the next activity.

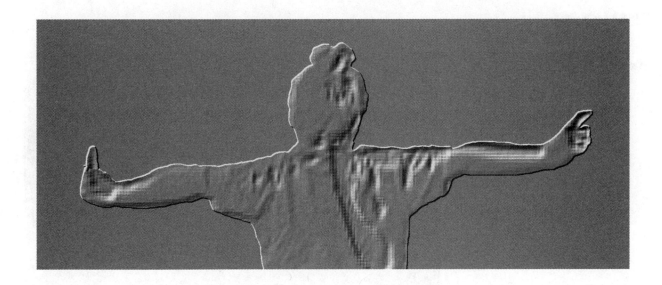

SURVIVAL

CONSIDER THE **PEDESTRIAN** IN **NEW YORK** CITY. CERTAINLY NO ONE WOULD **DESCRIBE** **CROSSING** THE STREET IN **NEW YORK** CITY AS A "LEISURELY" **ACTIVITY** AND **LIVE** TO TELL ABOUT IT.

ACTIVITY 1.3: I SEE, THEREFORE I AM

Ask the child why she thinks she sees. Why does she have eyes? Her answer will be: to see things, of course! But why does she need to see things? Why did human beings develop eyes and the kind of sight that she has? Answer: survival.

Why does the child see the moving fingers more easily than the steady fingers? The eyes are geared to respond to objects in motion more readily than static objects simply because if it's moving, you may need to deal with it quickly in order to survive. If it's static, it doesn't catch your attention as easily. You can then deal with whatever it is "at your leisure."

NEW YORK CITY

TAKING IT ALL IN ←————————————————

What we see is a composite of our peripheral vision and our small but sharply focused point of centricity. When you enter a room, your eye scans the entire scene, taking in bits of information in sharp focus, at the rate of hundreds of images per second.

At the same time that you are using your point of centricity, you are also utilizing peripheral vision, weaving the two into your impression of the room. Thus, if you can scan an entire scene and take in the essential information, you can and will certainly pick up all the elements in an 8-by-10-inch photograph, not just those in the *dead* center.

IT'S ALL UP THERE

SOME **SCIENTISTS** TELL US THAT **HUMANS** HAVE JUST THE RIGHT NUMBER OF **SYNAPSES** IN THE BRAIN TO RECORD **VIRTUALLY EVERYTHING** THE EYES SEE. IT'S ALL UP THERE, BUT **RETRIEVING** IT IS THE **PROBLEM**. NOW, **WHERE** WAS I?

YOUR IMPRESSION

WE ALL **LOOK** AT THE SAME THINGS, YET **SEE DIFFERENT** THINGS.

Claude Monet, Impressionist painter

MONET AND HIS COMPATRIOTS—EDOUARD **MANET**, EDGAR **DEGAS**, AUGUST **RENOIR**, AND OTHERS—WERE GREATLY **INFLUENCED** BY THE INVENTION AND PROLIFERATION OF **PHOTOGRAPHY**. IT FREED THEM TO PRODUCE **IMPRESSIONS** OF WHAT THEY SAW. PAINTERS NO LONGER HAD TO **REPRODUCE** REALITY; THEY COULD LEAVE IT TO THE CAMERA TO **RECORD REALITY**, SINCE IT SEEMED TO ACCOMPLISH THIS TASK EXTREMELY WELL.

2 THROUGH THE EYES OF A CHILD

EMILY HORSY

I was driving downtown with my two-year-old daughter Emily when she said, "Horsy, horsy, Daddy." I knew that there were no horses in the downtown area, but I had learned to trust her unbiased seeing. Sure enough, looking around I spotted a beautiful cloud in the shape of a horse. In this crucial teaching/parenting moment, if I had not been willing to respect her observational powers, then I would have "corrected" her, asserting that there were no horses present. This could have caused her to stop trusting her senses and her imagination. Instead, we celebrated her powers together!

⟶ **WHEN DO WE SEE BEST?**

If you ask a child at what age he thinks human beings see the best, he will often answer, "between sixteen and eighteen years old." This is probably because he perceives that in his late teens he will be grown up, capable of making many of his own decisions, controlling his own life.

I'LL SEE IT WHEN I BELIEVE IT

THIS STATEMENT **GRACES** THE **WALL** OF THE FIFTH-GRADE CLASSROOM OF

MASTER EDUCATOR JAY SHARP. IF YOU **EXPECT** TO SEE **SOMETHING**,

THE **ODDS** ARE THAT YOU **WILL SEE** IT, WHETHER IT'S **REALLY** THERE OR NOT.

Let's work together, taking what we have learned so far to come up with the correct answer. First, remember that the purpose of sight is survival, figuring out what your surroundings are all about, what hurts and what feels good, what is comforting and what is dangerous. All of the senses are employed toward this end. Second—and we are going to visit this again and again—prejudice plays an important part in determining to what degree we utilize our senses accurately.

Seeing is a complex weave of impressions formed by the action of light on the light-sensitive nerve endings in the retina. Then, and here's the rub, the brain takes over to interpret these sensations. Each individual uses his own experience to formulate his own impression of what he is seeing, making seeing an intensely personal experience.

At what age do most humans peak as far as using their sense of sight accurately? At what age do we have the least number of preconceived notions? The answer is: When we're very young. When we are young, we work actively with our sense of sight to figure it all out, to "survive." Almost everything interests or threatens us. The very young are constantly experimenting and processing information.

It is obvious now. *The very young see—and use all of their senses—the best.*

Note: That the very young see best is *generally* true. Anyone who uses his senses in an unprejudiced manner will see well. And, of course, you can learn to use your senses better at any age, or you might as well recycle the paper in this book for something useful!

UNPREJUDICED SEEING.
MARTINA, CENTRAL PARK, NEW YORK

ACTIVITY 2.1: YELLOW SUN?

1. Ask the child, "What color is the sun?" He may reply, "Yellow." Most people do.

2. Go outside with the child and briefly (more than one second can be harmful) look at the sun. You will see that it is white.

The sun emits all the wavelengths of light—red, orange, yellow, green, blue, indigo, and violet—that our eyes can register, along with infrared and ultraviolet, which they can't. We see this mix of all the wavelengths in the visible spectrum as white light.

The sun does not appear white at sunset and sunrise when its light reaches us at a severe angle, thus traveling through a greater density of the earth's atmosphere. The shorter wavelengths, with more peaks and valleys (the blue end of the spectrum), are more likely to be bent (refracted) by the earth's atmosphere, so they don't make it through to our eyes at sunset. Thus, a disproportionate quantity of light from the long wavelengths (red, yellow) makes it through to us and, voila! we see a red or yellow sunset.

JIMMY SAL, CANYONLANDS NATIONAL PARK, UTAH

WHAT COLOR IS YOUR SUN?

UNFORTUNATELY, I HAVE **SEEN** ELEMENTARY **SCHOOL** WORKBOOKS THAT **ASK CHILDREN** TO COMPLETE THIS SENTENCE: THE **COLOR** OF THE **SUN IS** _ _ _ _ _ _. UNABLE TO **ANSWER** THIS **SIMPLE QUESTION** I WENT TO THE **TEACHER'S** EDITION, **ONLY** TO FIND THE **ANSWER**: **YELLOW**. WRONG.

ACTIVITY 2.2: BE THE WAVELENGTH

Here's a critical-thinking-skill exercise that illustrates why the blue wavelengths—the short ones, with more peaks and valleys—are more likely to be bent by particles in the atmosphere than are the long red ones.

1. Put the child in the corner of the room that is farthest from the door. Tell him that someone has randomly scattered ten four-inch land mines across the floor.

2. The child must now find the safest route to the door. He must stay on the floor.

Many children will take circuitous, serpentine routes in an effort to make it safely. However, the correct course of action would be to take giant steps in a straight line directly to the door. Neither method guarantees success; but, the person who touches the floor the least number of times has the greatest chance of survival. Remember, the mines have been scattered randomly. Many people will prejudice the issue and have less chance of surviving by assuming that they must out-think the mind of the dreaded evil mine-layer.

ACTIVITY 2.3: COLORED LIGHTS

1. Ask the child the color of the lights in the room. The answer will probably be "white."

2. Ask the child to go outside just after sunset and look from a distance into some occupied buildings, noting the color of the lights.

He will see that the lights are yellow-orange if tungsten (ordinary) bulbs are in use. Fluorescent light bulbs will appear to be green. These light sources are not evenly balanced "sunlight"-quality white light. Each has its own particular wavelength bias, orange or green.

3. Question the child concerning why he originally saw the light as white. His prejudice, expecting to see white light, influenced him.

4. Ask the child why he had to go outside to see the real color of the light. In the early evening, there is just about as much light inside as out so the difference in color can be easily seen.

IF I ASK A **CLASS** OF **KINDERGARTEN** CHILDREN TO TELL ME THE **COLOR** OF THE

SKY, THEY REPLY WITH **RED**, **BLUE**, PINK, **YELLOW**, WHITE, AND **ALL** THE

OTHER **COLORS** THAT THE SKY **APPEARS** AT **ONE TIME** OR ANOTHER.

IF I PUT THE **SAME QUESTION** TO A **FOURTH-GRADE** CLASS,

UNFORTUNATELY THEY **ANSWER** "BLUE." PERIOD.

UNPREJUDICED SEEING

We have learned that, generally speaking, young children see the best. (They also use their senses of touch, taste, hearing, and smell more effectively than do most adults. Consequently, if a young child smells smoke, look for the fire.) They are not burdened by preconceived notions of what they think they should see. Also, they use their senses *actively*.

EYEWITNESS ACCOUNT

In attempting to learn from people who use the sense of sight in their work, I found myself talking to police investigators. They told me that when they need information from an eyewitness, they usually try to get the person to go into a state of deep relaxation. Relying on the belief that everything we see is recorded somewhere in the brain, the police want to access the witness's subconscious to get an accurate description of what took place. Otherwise, a witness tends to paint a visual report of characters and events that he thinks fit the particular crime.

The Relationship of Language to Unprejudiced Seeing

Studies suggest that our penchant for attaching words to things often limits the way we perceive those things. Of course, it all depends on the nature of the words (Mrs. versus Ms.). Research and common sense also suggest that language embodies the worldview of a culture. For example, a society's language may not include words that identify specific units of time such as minutes and seconds. That culture, in turn, is probably not concerned with being exactly on time. Its social and business relationships do not depend on the precise measurement or tracking of time.

Closure: I'll See It When I Believe It

Closure describes the act of assigning a certain value or judgment to something. This enables the individual to go about the business of living with some given assumptions. When used appropriately, closure is not a bad thing. It's important to recognize that a speeding car is more dangerous than one moving slowly, and that a red light always means STOP. But, does a green light always mean GO? A good defensive driver realizes that it only means GO when the drivers faced with the red light have decided to stop. Defensive driving means being aware, not taking anything for granted, making no assumptions or pre-conceived judgments.

The person who sees the best—uses his sense of sight to gather accurate information—is comfortable with uncertainty and ambiguity. That person does not prejudge and thus is actively using his senses. Remember, the

SNOW

ESKIMOS HAVE OVER **TWENTY**

VERY SPECIFIC **WORDS** TO

DESCRIBE A **SNOWSTORM**.

Peter Farb, Man's Rise

to Civilization

sense of sight has developed primarily as a survival mechanism. The person who uses his sight well is not only comfortable with uncertainty, but relies on it to a certain extent. The defensive driver is more likely to live longer, to survive.

THE POWER OF ONE

THE **VISUALLY LITERATE** PERSON **RESPECTS** THE POWER OF **CLOSURE** (PREJUDICE). THIS PERSON **UNDERSTANDS** THE **WISDOM** OF FREQUENTLY AND CONSTRUCTIVELY **EXAMINING PRECONCEIVED** NOTIONS.

ACTIVITY 2.4: IT'S ALL RELATIVE

1. Throw a ball straight up and catch it. The child should observe that it went straight up and down.

2. Now walk while you throw the same ball and catch it. The child will observe that the ball left your hand over one spot on the floor and returned to your hand at another. Although to you, the thrower-catcher, the ball seemed to travel straight up and down, its flight made a definite arc when viewed from the child's point of reference.

3. Have the child do the same activity while he is a passenger in a moving automobile or school bus. He should observe that the ball comes straight back to his hand, while at the same time actually traveling in an arc over the ground.

What happens when the car turns while the ball is in the air? The relative frames of reference change, and the ball does not return to the thrower's hand. This is relativity!

Oh, by the way, even when you stand still and toss the ball up, it is also traveling with momentum and therefore not in a straight line. Always remember that the earth is moving.

And Now for the Theory of Relativity

And so we come to Albert Einstein's Theory of Relativity. In the universe that scientists (those who seek knowledge) can comprehend today, relativity rules.

Simply put, there are no absolutes. Relativity, reality—the basic tenet is that we know things only in reference, in comparison, to other things. I'm big or small depending upon my dancing partner. I'm tall compared to someone shorter; I'm short compared to someone taller.

LIGHT BEHAVES AS BOTH A PARTICLE AND A WAVE. THINK OF PARTICLE ENERGY AS A TENNIS BALL BEING SERVED. IT ACTUALLY PICKS UP ENERGY BY BEING STRUCK, THEN IT TRAVELS ACROSS THE COURT DELIVERING THAT ENERGY TO THE RACQUET OF THE RECEIVER, WHO CAN FEEL HOW HARD THE SERVE WAS HIT. WAVE ENERGY IS FELT AT THE END OF A JUMP ROPE OR WHIP. A WAVE IS CREATED WHEN THE ENERGY GENERATED AT ONE END OF THE ROPE PASSES THROUGH THE PARTICLES OF THE ROPE TO THE OTHER END. EACH PARTICLE OF THE ROPE TRANSFERS THE ENERGY TO THE NEXT PARTICLE. THE PARTICLES THEMSELVES DON'T MOVE TO THE FAR END OF THE ROPE WITH THIS ENERGY, THOUGH THEY DO MOVE UP AND DOWN IN A WAVE PATTERN. IT IS DIFFICULT TO COMPREHEND HOW LIGHT CAN BE BOTH A PARTICLE AND A WAVE, EVEN THOUGH WE CAN PROVE THAT IT IS. THUS, AT THE HIGHEST LEVELS OF HUMAN KNOWLEDGE, UNCERTAINTY SEEMS TO BE THE ONLY CERTAINTY!

Notice in Activity 2.3 that to approach any level of truth, it was necessary to look from another frame of reference (outside just after sunset) to appreciate the actual color of the light in the room. By the way, once this prejudice concerning the inside light is broken, you can actually see the real color, even when surrounded by it.

THE ZEN CHECKER

My computer's spell-checker will allow me to spell judgment *with an* e *between the* g *and the* m, *or without. Baffled by this, I learned that the extra* e *is permitted in British-English (English-English?). I like to think that I have a Zen spell-checker; it will not make a judgment about the word* judgment! *Trackers—experts at utilizing their sense of sight—tell me that frame of mind is important, that they do their best with an open mind. If they are looking only for the footprints of a child lost in the woods, they may miss a piece of torn clothing on a tree branch. They trust the eye's ability to take in vast amounts of information, and they attempt to keep their perceptions and minds open to all possibilities.*

ACTIVE SEEING VS. PASSIVE VIEWING

We can all learn to see actively again, and we can encourage our children to retain their visual skills. This can profoundly affect our appreciation of life. Seeing is not lost forever as we grow up; rather, it seems to become dormant as we stop actively utilizing it. *By simply looking again, we immediately start to see again.*

We certainly spend a good deal of time looking at, being influenced by, and possibly making two-dimensional images. However, the majority of our visual effort is simply spent looking at, seeing, the world around us.

Active seeing means using the information that the sense of sight provides to your brain. The active seer questions, compares, and is conscious and aware. Once we have gotten into the habit of being passive viewers, it takes some work, a conscious, pleasurable effort, to break this bad habit. Remember, by fourth grade children were saying that the sky is blue, period. *Passive viewing* is all about taking your sense of sight for granted.

VISUAL RELATIONSHIPS.
COLUMBUS AVENUE, NEW YORK CITY

ACTIVITY 2.5 DO YOU SEE WHAT I SEE?

1. Ask the child to take a few minutes and find five things in his immediate surroundings that he has never seen before. As his eye rapidly scans the scene, he probably finds nothing new. The purpose of this activity is to look actively for things never noticed.

The child may notice:

Things: a box in the corner, a hat on a clothes tree, a new or old car in a neighbor's driveway

Relationships: a bush that has grown to be twice as big as it used to be, the fact that the street gradually curves to the right a few blocks away, a seldom-used chair that has been moved to a different location in the living room

Qualities: the way that the light streams through the bedroom window, how pale and soft the blue bathroom walls are, the way the leaves of a particular tree blow in the wind ("the answer my friend")

Rhythms: repetition of a theme—the slats on the blinds, the bricks in the wall, the tiles on the bathroom floor

2. Discuss and appreciate the observations together, along with your newly increased awareness.

APPRECIATE

TO **RECOGNIZE** THE VALUE, THE QUALITY, OR THE **SIGNIFICANCE**

OF **PEOPLE** OR THINGS; TO BE **AWARE** OF

IN THE FUTURE **ARTISTS** WILL JUST **POINT**.

Marcel Duchamp, Surrealist artist

GATEWAY ARCH, ST. LOUIS, AND DELICATE ARCH, UTAH

You have just completed the most important lesson in this entire book. Now, when you are with the child, encourage a continuing process of inquiry starting with:
"Do you notice that?"
"Look what I see."
"Why do you think that's there?"

ACTIVE SEEING

CONSCIOUSLY USING YOUR VISION BEYOND WHAT YOU

NEED TO SURVIVE WILL GREATLY ENRICH YOUR LIFE AND

ACTUALLY LEAD YOU TO VISUAL LITERACY ON YOUR OWN.

ACTIVITY 2.6: TRAINING FOR ACTIVE SEEING

1. In this activity you will learn to "bulk up" the "perceptual muscles." Have the child look at a distant scene, taking it all in (the mountains in the distance, the plains, or a cityscape).

2. He should now focus on a particular element in the scene (a particular group of trees, or a particular building).

3. Have the child describe the characteristics of this particular element down to the most minute detail possible.

4. Now relate these details to the entire scene as viewed in step 1. Notice how it all fits together.

The whole is equal to the sum of its parts.

PARTICULAR

A SPECIFIC **PERSON**,

GROUP, OR **THING**;

NOT GENERAL; **DETAIL**

New York City

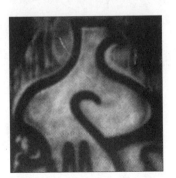

"ELEMENTARY, MY DEAR WATSON"

ARTHUR CONAN DOYLE'S **SHERLOCK HOLMES**, ONE OF THE GREAT **ACTIVE SEERS**, USES **DEDUCTIVE REASONING** TO SOLVE HIS CASES. DEDUCING **REQUIRES** APPROACHING A PROBLEM WITH AN **OPEN MIND**—ELIMINATING ONLY WHAT IS **IMPOSSIBLE** AND KEEPING ALL THE OTHER POSSIBILITIES **OPEN**.

3 PHOTOGRAPHY: THE BASICS

THIS IS NOT A TREE

THE PHOTOGRAPH

A photograph is a drawing on paper (graph) made with light (photo): a light-drawing (not a heavy drawing—although they can clearly communicate "heavy" concepts). Thus, a photograph is a drawing that is made using light. Sometimes we make drawings using pencils, crayons, or paint. In a photograph, we use the energy of the light to make the drawing.

WHAT'S IN A WORD?

WHY DO YOU THINK

THE **LEAD** IN **PENCILS**

IS CALLED **GRAPHITE**?

RESPONSIBILITY

One morning I was passing out cameras to a fourth-grade class. I wanted them to handle the cameras with care, so I asked them to tell me what the word responsibility meant. Much to my surprise (and delight) hands immediately shot up, and one student shouted, "It means the ability to respond."

Of course this teacher, and her students, were way ahead of me. She had taught them that the best way to understand words is to break them up into any component parts and then guess at the meaning of these parts. Responsibility—"the ability to respond." I never heard it put so well. Now that's word power!

Camera and Film:
The Physical Process

These basics of photography are all that you need to know—maybe more than you need to know—to work with the photographic image. The light enters the camera (derived from the Greek word for *room*) through a small opening in the lens. Whenever light passes through a small opening, it actually forms an image. The light hits the film (made primarily of silver, which has consistent qualities when reacting with light), literally burning the image onto the film with its energy. In most cases this is a latent image (it's there, but we can't see it, yet); electrons have been knocked around responding to different colors and intensities of light. However, we must develop the film to see the image made by the light.

Film processing has two basic stages:
1. Development: In total darkness, the film is immersed in a chemical solution to complete the reaction with the light so that we can see it. This product can be in negative or positive (slides, transparencies) form.
2. Fixing: Still in total darkness, the film is immersed in a chemical that removes all of the remaining silver that could react with light. It is now safe to view in the light.

You may have an image in your mind of photographers working under an orange safe-light. However, safe-lights are not used for developing film since most film responds to all the colors of light, including orange. They are used when enlarging and printing black and white photographs on special paper that does not respond to orange-yellow light (orthochromatic paper as opposed to panchromatic film).

→ THE PHOTOGRAPHIC LANGUAGE

Photography is a language; a photograph is representational information that is used to communicate. It is not to be taken literally, but translated into its accepted meaning. Take another look at the photograph on page 39. It is different shapes and shades of gray that are translated to represent the concept of "tree."

REPRESENTATION

THINK ABOUT THE **WORD** REPRESENTATION. IT HAS **TWO PARTS:**

RE AND PRESENTATION, MEANING **TO PRESENT SOMETHING**

TO YOU FOR **ANOTHER** LOOK, A **DIFFERENT** LOOK.

ACTIVITY 3.1: THE CAMERA OBSCURA

This is a good time to introduce the famous *camera obscura* ("dark chamber") for a deeper, sensory-level understanding of how the camera, and the human eye, work. Kids of all ages love this one.

1. Find a room with only one window that looks out on a bright, sunny scene. Cover the window with black paper so that the room is relatively dark when you turn off the lights.

2. Make a small hole about 1/8 inch in diameter in the paper.

3. Hold up a piece of white paper twelve to eighteen inches from the hole. On the side of the paper facing the hole, you will see whatever is outside the window, in full color!

If you are working in a classroom, do the best you can to achieve darkness. The image can still be seen and can have a profound effect on your students, even if there are numerous light leaks.

Whenever light passes through a small opening, it forms an image. As the opening gets larger, the image gets brighter, but less focused, blurrier. Light rays from a particular point (the very top of a tree) pass through a larger opening at different angles, striking the paper across a greater area than a smaller opening would permit. Experiment with the aperture size of your camera obscura.

A lens is used to bend the light. The rays of light from an object hit the lens and bend to meet at a particular point of focus, the film. At a time of weakness in your youth, you may have used a lens to gather light from the sun and focus it on some poor unsuspecting insect.

This is how the camera works. This is how your eye works. In your eye, you have a lens covering the opening called the *pupil,* and the light-sensitive nerves in your retina act as the film.

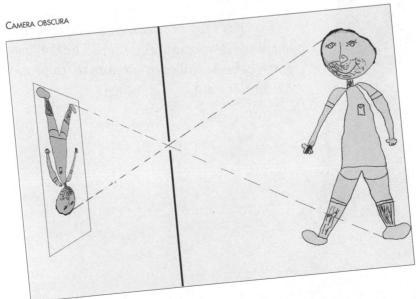

CAMERA OBSCURA

The sounds in a particular language are not to be taken literally, but rather are endowed with particular meaning within that language:

"I love you." These are only sounds if you don't know the English language.

"Te amo." These are only sounds if you don't know the Spanish language.

Some sounds, of course, are basically literal, real, not representational: a window shattering. These may also have some attendant meaning: Heather has a lousy throwing arm, and, there goes her allowance.

If you write "I love you" on a blackboard, what is it really? It's chalk, a kind of crushed stone, on slate, another type of stone. But when you can read the written language and have an understanding of its symbols, "I love you" takes on an entirely different reality—a deep feeling, a strong bond between two human beings.

The English language has certain rules of grammar to ensure clear communication. The language of photography also has rules of "grammar" to promote effective communication.

THIS IS NOT A STOP SIGN(S).

ACTIVITY 3.2: PHOTOGRAPHY AS A LANGUAGE

Look at the light-drawing (photograph) above. Ask the child what it is. More than likely the answer will be "rocks."

Of course, these are not rocks. It is a photograph, a light-drawing. It is, in fact, a light-drawing on "a slice of tree" (paper)!

Why is this seemingly obvious realization so important? Because most people are unaware of the obvious. Most people will respond, "rocks."

Where does it "become" rocks? In your mind. You have prior experience recognizing rocks, and you understand that photographs are derived from reality. Thus, you know that this is a light-drawing of rocks.

Big deal. Well, in the context of what you are attempting to learn or teach, it is a big deal. It means that Photography Is a Language.

By learning the rules of grammar of this language, you will be better able to understand it and use it to communicate effectively.

THE VOCABULARY OF PHOTOGRAPHY

Point of View

A *dimension* is simply a measurement. Visual imagery is generally expressed in two dimensions, height and width. The third dimension, depth, although present in sculpture, is missing or implied in photographs, paintings, and even on the television or a movie screen. Time is the fourth dimension that we need to consider to describe reality accurately. (We will look more closely at time later.) Thus, to know something's exact measurements in space you must know its height, width, depth, and when it was there, or its movement (time).

A photograph is a two-dimensional representation of our four-dimensional reality. It uses what is called a single viewpoint: The shapes and angles of a three-dimensional object in the photograph represent that object from a single point of view (POV). It doesn't matter from what angle you look at the photograph, your view will still be locked into that of the photographer at the moment she made the picture. Remember that the photographer decides the viewer's point of view. This is also true for a drawing made using a single point of view. (The *Mona Lisa* always looks directly at you, making eye contact with you. You can't shake her.)

Perspective

Perspective is the technique we use to render
three-dimensional objects on two-dimensional paper.
Photographic perspective uses a single point of view with
vanishing point(s) that converge on the horizon line.

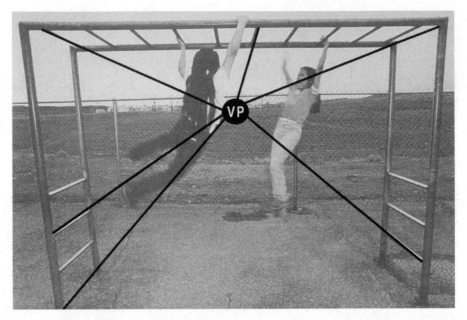

PHOTOGRAPHIC PERSPECTIVE

The use of perspective in Western art has been greatly influenced by the camera obscura. From the Renaissance on, painters began to explore perspective, learning how to add depth to their works by making lines converge on the horizon, just like the image formed by the camera obscura.

Our eye functions like the camera obscura, so we are very comfortable with the idea of a single point of view and converging perspective, so much so that if we are faced with a painting or photographic manipulation that does not render three dimensions in this way, we consider it "unrealistic."

MULTIPLE POINTS OF VIEW:
CUBIST PHOTOMONTAGE

CUBISM AND REALITY

AROUND 1906 PABLO **PICASSO** AND GEORGES **BRAQUE** DEVELOPED A NEW **STYLE** OF

PAINTING. **CUBISM**, SO CALLED BECAUSE OF THE **SHAPES** THAT DOMINATED THE

PAINTINGS, WAS AN ATTEMPT TO RENDER **REALITY** ON A **FLAT** CANVAS. **CUBISTS**

PAINTED THE SAME **SUBJECT** FROM THREE OR FOUR DIFFERENT **VIEWS**, LAYERING THEM

ON TOP OF **ONE ANOTHER**. ALTHOUGH THIS **TECHNIQUE** IS GENERALLY CONSIDERED AN

ABSTRACTION OF REALITY, THESE PAINTERS FELT IT MORE ACCURATELY **TRANSLATED**

DYNAMIC REALITY TO CANVAS THAN THE STATIC, SINGLE **POINT OF VIEW**

THAT WAS **PREVALENT** IN MOST PAINTINGS AT THE TIME.

FROM THE PERSPECTIVE OF A FIFTEENTH-CENTURY PAINTER

PHOEBE-LOU ADAMS, **REVIEWING** *PIERO DELLA FRANCESCA* BY RONALD LIGHTBROWN

(ABBEVILLE, 1992) FOR *ATLANTIC* MAGAZINE, **COMMENTS**, "MR. LIGHTBROWN'S TEXT

CONCENTRATES ON [DELLA FRANCESCA'S] WORK . . . ABOVE ALL, THE **SUBTLE**

SHIFTS OF **PERSPECTIVE** THE PAINTER EMPLOYED TO **CREATE**

THE ILLUSION OF REALISTIC SPACE BY UNREALISTIC MEANS."

(Atlantic, March 1993)

BOB AND JIM, WILLIAMSTOWN, MASSACHUSETTS

Foreground and Background

Because two-dimensional imagery is considered to have no depth, objects near the camera as well as those far away from the camera, and everything in between, come together on one surface, the photograph. Visual clues (the grammar and syntax of visual literacy) help us add depth, or the third dimension, to photographs and drawings. This addition is done in our heads. The mind pretends that there is a third dimension. Remember, photography is a language—the third dimension is representational along with the rest of "reality" as expressed in the photograph.

Look at the photograph to the right. These are not trees, but a photograph, a light-drawing that we read and translate into "trees"! You can read it in one of two ways, either

1. the trees are radically different in size, or
2. the trees are the same size but some are farther in the distance than others.

Because we are familiar with looking at two-dimensional imagery and adding depth, we would read the photo the second way: The trees are the same size, but they are different distances away from the viewer.

LITERAL

AN EXACT **READING**, AVOIDING

METAPHOR OR **EMBELLISHMENT**

Translating what the image means, what it is communicating to us on the physical level, we read "trees, forest." It may also be saying something on other levels about freedom, love, or nature's goodness, but for the moment let's just stay with the physical, literal interpretation.

THERE IS **REALLY** NOTHING **TWO-DIMENSIONAL** IN OUR **WORLD**; EVERY PAGE

OR PHOTO DOES HAVE SOME **THICKNESS**, A **THIRD** DIMENSION. HOWEVER,

CONCEPTUALLY, THE **IMAGE** ON THE **PAGE**, THE PHOTO, IS A

TWO-DIMENSIONAL REPRESENTATION OF **REALITY**.

ACTIVITY 3.3: THE HANDY CAM

This activity will enable you to provide a viewing tool, a camera with many different lenses, to your child at absolutely no cost. Better yet this "camera" will always be with her.

1. Have the child extend the index finger and thumb of each hand.

2. Next, have her join the tip of the thumb of one hand to the tip of the thumb of the other. She should overlap the knuckles of her index fingers to form a rectangular frame.

3. The child should extend her arms, close one eye, and look through her new "handy camera."

4. Now tell the child to say thank you, because you have just given her a camera with an unlimited supply of film.

Here's how it works. (Technical ability is not required.) The hands form the shape of a rectangle, the traditional picture frame format. Through this frame, the child looks at the world, and she can point out

what she thinks would make good photographs. By doing so, she is sharpening her active viewing skills, as well as her sense of composition, the grammar of visual literacy.

The Handy Cam is a great tool to share with the child: "Look what I see," and "Look at the nice photograph I could make."

Caution: Just as you should never walk while looking through the viewfinder of a camera, it is dangerous to walk around looking through the Handy Cam. Look first; then, when you see something interesting, stop and put the Handy Cam to your eye. Remember that the Handy Cam is simply a tool. Seeing is done best with both eyes (as well as ears, nose, tongue, and skin) and at all times.

HANDY CAM

A POLE IN THE HEAD

ACTIVITY 3.4: FOREGROUND AND BACKGROUND

1. Hold up the photograph of the trees on page 51. Ask the child which lines are in the back and which lines are in the front. When she answers that the big trees are in the front and the smaller ones are in the back, point out to her that the page in the book has almost no thickness and the lines that she is reading as trees are all sharing the same surface. There are none in the front and none in the back! Remind her that these are not trees, but a light-drawing. (One of my third-grade students,

Jack, got so tired of me saying this that one day he corrected me. He told me, and the rest of the class, that the page in the book was in reality a slice of tree after all!)

2. Have the child use her Handy Cam or, if a real camera is available, make a photograph that fills the frame with what she wants (always!) and also exhibits that she is paying attention to the foreground/background relationship.

3. Critique the image with the child. Is it clear that some objects

are in front and others in back? How do we know what was in front, closer to her camera, in the real scene, and what was in back?

We know by obscurity. The element that obscures, or blocks, another element is the one in front.

We also know by the size that objects appear to be in the photo and our prior knowledge of what things are larger than others in reality.

A POLE IN THE HEAD

ATTENTION MUST BE PAID TO THE **RELATIONSHIP** BETWEEN THE **SUBJECT**

(ALSO CALLED THE FIGURE) AND THE **SURROUNDINGS** (THE GROUND).

OTHERWISE, TELEPHONE **POLES** SEEM TO **SPROUT** FROM THE **HEADS** OF PEOPLE!

THIN SOLDIERS

Beware—prior knowledge can also be used against you. For example, an advertiser can persuade you that a product is larger than it really is by using realistic models in a deceptive composition. I've never been able to forget the disappointment I felt years ago when the soldiers I ordered from an ad on the back of my Superman magazine arrived. I was crushed to find that the figures were only an inch high and paper thin! Despite what I said about everything having a third dimension, I think these things were 2-D. (There went a week's worth of newspaper delivery money!)

Depth of Field

Another term used in photography is *depth of field*, which refers to the minimum and maximum distances that will be in focus in a particular photograph. The size of the lens opening, the aperture, has an effect upon how much of the photograph is in focus. The smaller the lens opening, the greater the depth of field. The greater the depth of field, the greater the "thickness" of focus. For example, with a particular lens and a small opening, all objects that are five feet to fifteen feet from the camera may be in focus, giving you a depth of field of ten feet. Under all the same conditions, but with a larger lens opening, the depth of field may only be eight feet to ten feet from the camera, or only two feet in thickness.

Why not always use the smallest opening for more depth of field? Unfortunately, the smaller the opening, the less light gets through the lens and the slower the shutter speed required. As the shutter speed gets slower than 1/60th of a second, the image will begin to blur from camera movement (see Chapter 6, Time). A tripod is a very helpful tool; it keeps the camera steady so that you can use extremely slow shutter speeds for great depth of field. The only blur will occur if the object you are photographing—such as a four-year-old child—is moving.

Faster films (ASA 400 and higher) are more sensitive to light, permitting the use of a small aperture for greater depth of field with a relatively fast shutter speed for a minimum of blur.

You can use a small depth of field to accentuate a particular subject. If the subject is the only thing in focus, we read it to be extremely important.

SELECTIVE FOCUS. MONTEZUMA CREEK, UTAH

Size

Size is another grammatical element within the picture frame. Look at the photograph on the left.

Most people will say that in this photograph the child is big, or the child looks big. No one would assert that the child is actually bigger than the building, but the photograph definitely implies visually that we are dealing with a large, important child.

KING KONG SYNDROME: THE GIRL AS LARGE AS THE BUILDING. *NEW YORK CITY*

A C T I V I T Y   3 . 6 :   S U B J E C T   S I Z E

1. Select a photograph with a dominant subject. (You can use our example.)

2. Have the child list the elements in the photograph (example: child, building, sky, ground).

3. Have the child order the list by size. Start with the elements that take up the most space (area) in the photograph (example: child, sky, building, ground).

4. Ask the child the approximate percentage of the picture area covered by each element (example: child 20 percent; sky 30 percent; building 15 percent; and so on). If the child does not yet understand percentages, here is a great opportunity to learn.

To get at this without percentages, phrase the question in economic terms (the "money is everything" approach). Tell the child that the photograph costs $1; ask how many cents each element is worth based on its size.

Angle of View

Another grammatical element within the picture frame is the angle of view, illustrated below at right.

We are looking down on this child, and she is looking up at us. When we look up at something, we tend to respect it more; it is larger and more important to us. We use the phrase "look up to" as a term of respect. Conversely, looking down on someone or something engenders a feeling of disrespect or superiority on our part.

Looking up to

Looking down on

This also translates into body language, another primarily visual language. We bow to those we respect, so that we are looking up at them. Queens and kings have often made this mandatory because it's difficult to gain the upper hand when you are cowering on the ground.

Also, notice the "extra" headroom, space between the top of the subject and the frame. This is another conventional way of indicating a small subject. (Of course the space is not "extra." It is an important, intended element in the communication.) The converse is also true, if the top of the subject is near the top of the frame (appears "jammed into the frame"), this will make the subject seem larger.

ACTIVITY 3.7: ANGLE OF VIEW AND HEADROOM

1. Ask the child to make a photograph or drawing of something that is really quite small and unimposing. She should arrange her angle of view looking up at the object with tight headroom, so that it appears large and important. She can also use the Handy Cam for this activity.

2. Conversely, have the child make a two-dimensional image of something that in reality is quite large and imposing. Have her use an angle looking down on it and lots of headroom, to make it seem small and unimportant.

3. You can also experiment by having the child look at you while she is lying down on the ground. Then, sit on the ground and have the child get up on a chair and look down at you. Try this with any number of household or classroom things. Make photographs at these different angles, if you like.

Visual Grammar

Now that you are familiar with photography's lingo, we can move on to learning more about using your new vocabulary. Look at the drawing below. Notice that it is a picture of a person. Look at how little of the area is actually devoted to the person. This picture is really telling us that she is small (and perhaps unimportant).

SMALL, POSSIBLY UNIMPORTANT

ANASAZI RUINS, NEW MEXICO

MONEY IS EVERYTHING

THINK OF THE AREA OF A **PICTURE**

COSTING A **CERTAIN** AMOUNT PER

SQUARE **INCH**. LET'S SAY THE

ENTIRE PHOTO COSTS ONE **DOLLAR**.

THE **VISUALLY** LITERATE IMAGE

MAKER USES **EVERY** CENT OF THIS

DOLLAR. **WASTE NOT**, WANT NOT.

Now look at the photograph to the left. There is absolutely no doubt that the girl is the subject. Unfortunately, the overwhelming majority of photographs made in our society look like the first image. The subject is small and placed directly in the middle. You need only spend a few minutes looking at a friend's vacation snapshots to see that this is true. The reason is simple: Most people don't know the language of photography. They don't know how to re-present things photographically.

BAÑO

While in Mexico I found myself in desperate need of a bathroom. Not knowing Spanish, I looked in my travel dictionary and found the word baño. Next I searched—but not too hard for I was running out of time—for a kind-looking person. Finding one, which is easy in Mexico, I blurted out, "Baño, gracias, baño, gracias." Luckily he noticed my body language and pointed me in the right direction.

My helpful listener had to do all the work to figure out what I wanted. The same is true of someone looking at a poor photograph. After working at it a bit, the enlightened viewer might figure out what the photographer wanted to say.

Word power: communication, emphasis on the co, meaning that both sender and receiver work together. A photographer who handles her visual language poorly forces the viewer to do all of the work to figure out the communication, and there is no guarantee that this will happen.

4 FRAMING AN IMAGE

CRITICAL THINKING **SKILLS** (THINKING CRITICALLY) FORM THE **BASIS** FOR THIS

ENTIRE BOOK. TO CRITIQUE SIMPLY MEANS "**TO MAKE A JUDGMENT**" ABOUT SOMETHING.

THE TERM **CRITICAL** OFTEN

HAS A NEGATIVE CONNOTATION IN OUR **SOCIETY**. THIS IS SIMPLY NOT ACCURATE.

TO BE CRITICAL MEANS TO **EXAMINE** SOMETHING, TO LOOK AT IT, **TO PAY ATTENTION**

TO IT, AND **TO THINK** ABOUT IT CONSCIOUSLY.

FRAMING: A KEY ELEMENT OF VISUAL LITERACY

What is the most important part of a photograph?

A fourth grader answered this question brilliantly by saying, "the frame itself."

"Why the frame itself?" I inquired.

"Because the frame determines what is in the picture and what is not in the picture," she said. Exactly! I wish I had said it myself, and now I have.

DERKS FIELD, SALT LAKE CITY

Take a look at the photo above. Which is bigger, the policeman or the mountains? Based on the information given in the photo, you are tempted to answer, "They're about the same size!" Of course, you would not answer the question just from the information given in the photo alone. You have had experience with mountains and people, and from this experience you know that the mountain is probably much larger than the man. I say probably

FRAMING

FRAMING IS THE **ACT** OF

DETERMINING WHAT WILL

BE **CONSIDERED**.

WE FRAME A **QUESTION**,

WE **FRAME** OUR ANSWERS,

WE FRAME A **PICTURE**.

FROM THE FILM PROMISED LAND, SALT FLATS, UTAH

because it might be a small model mountain, not a real one, although this is unlikely. However, advertisers often use our preconceived ideas (our prejudices) about reality to control our judgments about their products.

The average person in our society tends to be functionally illiterate when it comes to photography. He can read it, that is decipher given visual information fairly well, but he can't speak it. He picks up the camera knowing what he wants to say about the subject that matters to him (the subject matter), but he doesn't know how to communicate it visually. He is relatively sure of what he wants to say, but he is unsure of the language. *Not knowing the language, he just wants to be sure that what he has to say, his subject, appears in the frame. So he positions the subject in the middle of the frame.* Like those who believed the earth to be flat in the fifteenth century, he doesn't want his subject to get close to the edge; it might fall off! By putting it directly in the middle, he feels confident that it will appear. And it does, but it's small and unimportant. In effect, he communicates exactly the opposite of what he wanted to say.

PAY ATTENTION

WHEN **MAKING**

A PHOTOGRAPH,

PAY **ATTENTION** TO

EACH AND EVERY **ELEMENT**

THAT **YOU** INCLUDE.

"GOD IS IN THE **DETAILS**."

Ludwig Mies van der Rohe, architect

TOOELE

I was working with some sixth graders in Tooele, Utah (really, look it up), as part of the National Endowment for the Arts Artists in Education program. The kids were using cameras I'd brought to school. One of them came running up to me excitedly saying, "John I don't got no film, I don't got no film!"

I responded by saying, "Feel free to go ahead and use all the rest of the film in the camera."

"But I don't got no film?"

"Go ahead and use the rest of it," I insisted.

The impasse continued, and he became convinced that I had a screw (or two) loose. At that point I asked him to write down exactly what he had said. We dissected and diagramed it together so that he could see that NOT having NO FILM literally meant that HE HAD FILM.

Okay, I knew what he meant, and in many languages other than English, double negatives do not equal positives. Poetic license aside, I felt that my role in that situation was to believe what the child was telling me, to take his communication at face value, to trust and respect him. This provided an excellent learning opportunity. I stressed that it's his language, and he can break the rules effectively only if he knows them. In fact, it related nicely to our lesson on making a good photograph—say what you mean.

It is really quite simple to become photographically literate instantly. The key is, as you may have already suspected: use the entire picture area. This communication skill can then be developed to higher and higher levels.

ACTIVITY 4.1: CROP IT

Give the child a magazine that contains some photographs. Be prepared to sacrifice it since he is going to cut it up and draw on it.

1. Have him pick out a photo that he likes.

2. Have the child write down all the things (elements) in the photo.

3. Now ask the child to order the elements from the most to the least important on the list.

4. Give the child a ruler and a pencil and have him draw a box somewhere on the original photo, singling out one of the elements on his list.

5. Have the child cut out this box.

6. Ask the child what it is. Remember, the first answer should always be "a photograph, a light-drawing." Getting past that, and hopefully having some fun with it,

discuss what the light-drawing in its present form is communicating. Value every answer; different things have different meanings to different people.

7. Critique the newly created image with the child. Is everything included that should be included? Is there anything in the image that should be excluded?

MONUMENT VALLEY HIGH SCHOOL, UTAH

FRAMING: WHAT TO LOOK FOR

Vertical and Horizontal

The Handy Cam (see Activity 3.3) can be used in either the vertical or horizontal format.

* The vertical view is referred to in "computerese" as *portrait* orientation. The shape of a human being often fits well into this view.
* The horizontal view is referred to as *landscape* orientation.

THE **FIRST** WORD

IN THE OLD **DICK AND JANE**

READERS IS **LOOK**.

VERTICAL, HEIGHT-RELATED, "FALLING" IMAGE.
CAPITAL REEF NATIONAL PARK, UTAH

As the child views and composes through the Handy Cam, ask him to make a conscious decision as to whether the frame is filled (composed better) in the horizontal or vertical format. Take neither for granted.

Wide-Angle View

With the Handy Cam held close to the eye, the angle of view is large. It contains many elements and is similar to a wide-angle lens on a camera.

WIDE-ANGLE VIEW. *UTAH*

Telephoto View

As the child moves his fingers farther from his eye, the angle of view narrows. With his arms fully outstretched, he is composing with only a very few elements in the frame.

Note: Through a telephoto lens the foreground and background of the picture appear very close to each other. The waterfall appears to be just behind the trees, while in reality they are quite a distance apart.

TELEPHOTO COMPRESSION OF FOREGROUND AND BACKGROUND.
YELLOWSTONE NATIONAL PARK, WYOMING

1. Ask the child to use his Handy Cam to make (find) three good photographs. He should look and see actively. Use the word *make* rather than *take*. *Make* implies a concerted effort on the part of the photographer, the child.

2. Give the child one limitation: include no people in these first photos. Encourage him to use the entire picture area.

Why no people? Photography was invented between 1829 and 1839, more or less simultaneously by many people, among them an Englishman, William Henry Fox Talbot, and a Frenchman, Joseph Niepce. Historians tell us that by 1850 half of the humans in the world had had their pictures taken! The idea of a "realistic" image of one's self was (and still is) extremely compelling.

Most people have a prejudice concerning photography: they think first of pictures of people—look at the advertisements for cameras and film. Asking the child to make a photo rather than to take a picture of someone gets the wheels spinning in his head.

As noted in Chapter 1, each prejudice provides a wonderful opportunity for a teacher or parent. By using the prejudice, you can open a closed mind.

3. Have the child describe the three photographs to you. This is a great communication exercise. It plays upon the act of translating the real world from one form of language (visual) to another (oral/written). Here are some ideas for working with the child and his descriptions.

Verbal Description

Encourage the child to be precise in his language so that both of you can "see" the photograph. When he finishes his verbal description, look at his proposed photograph.

Critique his verbal description. You may find that he has made a very nice photograph, but his verbalization is poor. You can then use the visual literacy he possesses to help him with his verbal literacy.

If, on the other hand, he describes a very nice image in words, but his Handy Cam composition is weak—not visually well expressed—work with him to improve his visual communication skills, his visual literacy. Help him be aware of, and pay attention to, everything contained in the frame.

To make the child more aware of his visual literacy, ask if the "photograph" works better as a horizontal or a vertical. Then ask if the "photograph" would improve with less (telephoto) or more (wide angle) things in it. Remember—and remind him—that less is often more.

Written Description

As with the Navajo kids in the introduction of this book, I have found that children who hate to write will often gladly attempt to write about the visual images they've made or seen and by doing so discover the possibilities in written communication. Take the child through the same steps outlined above, asking him to write down his description rather than verbalize it.

(Continued on next page)

SEE WRITE

NEVER TRY TO **WRITE**

UNTIL **YOU** CAN SEE

WHAT YOU ARE **GOING**

TO **WRITE** ABOUT.

Timothy Gangwer, master writing

teacher and author,

speaking to a fourth-grade class

ACTIVITY 4.2: CONTINUED

Pictorial Description

Have the child make rough pencil drawings showing the basic structures of his visual images. This is similar to diagraming a sentence. Match up these drawings with the child's images. How close are the drawings to the Handy Cam images?

Use the drawings and the imaginary photographs to reinforce the basic principle of filling the frame efficiently to communicate clearly.

4. Together with the child, assign each of his three composed

imaginary images, each "photograph," to one of the following groups:

Group One: The images in this group say more or less what the child wanted to communicate. They are grammatically correct in terms of visual literacy.

Group Two: These photos do not utilize the picture area effectively, and the subject is not clearly expressed. They are grammatically incorrect in terms of visual literacy.

TEACHER/AUTHOR TIM GANGWER IN CLASSROOM, BASSAM, IVORY COAST

BRONX, NEW YORK

1. If you have access to a camera, repeat exercise 4.2 with the child. This time, however, have him make actual photographs. Any camera will work, but an instant camera or a still-video camera is best. The sooner you can see the photos after they have been taken, the better.

Note: At this point, do not be concerned with the technical qualities of the photos, such as the focus, lightness and darkness, or print quality. The child will naturally want to improve these things to make his communication stronger.

2. Ask the child what he was attempting to communicate, the subject matter. Do the photos include everything necessary to make their points efficiently? Do unnecessary things in the photos detract from the message?

3. Have the child put the photos into two groups:

Group One: These say more or less what the child wanted to communicate. These are grammatically correct in terms of visual literacy.

Group Two: These photos do not utilize most of the picture area effectively, or use the entire frame. They are grammatically incorrect in terms of visual literacy.

DEAR TEACHER, PLEASE
STAY.ON YOUR TOES

A child once showed me a photo she had made in which what appeared to be her subject (a car) was quite small and directly in the middle—a classic poor photograph. (There are no bad photographs, since you can always learn something from them.)

However, when I asked her what she had intended to picture, she replied, "Sky up above, mountains in the back, three trees on the left, the school on the right, and a car in the middle." Her photo was exactly what she wanted. It was grammatically correct even though it appeared to be an example of poor visual grammar.

Sometimes what appears to be the main subject of a photo may be small, along with many other elements in the picture, and it can still be grammatically correct, if the photographer intended it to be so.

THE IMPORTANCE OF THE ENTIRE FRAME

In this age of instant information, we are bombarded with images. We often seem to follow a sequence when we look at visual information:

1. The eyes randomly scan the entire scene, noticing large shapes and patterns.

2. The quality of the image and its composition begin to drive the scanning.
3. Focused vision now comes into play concentrating on areas of interest.

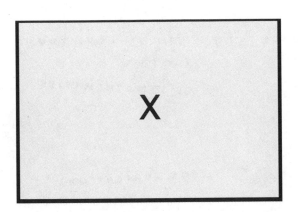

"X" DOES NOT MARK THE SPOT

"X" MARKS THE SPOT—THE ENTIRE FRAME COUNTS

A C T I V I T Y   4 . 3 :   X   M A R K S   T H E   S P O T

1. Draw a rectangle to represent an empty photographic frame.

2. Ask the child to put an X on the most important part of the frame. This is nearly impossible since each part of the frame is equally important. If you have successfully completed the previous activities in this book, you are going to have a rightfully reluctant child on your hands. No "one spot" is more important than another.

I say that this is nearly impossible because I have had some creative children mark an X over the entire frame!

THE WHOLE EQUALS THE SUM OF ITS PARTS

WHAT IS THE MOST **IMPORTANT** PART OF YOUR LIFE, THE BEGINNING, THE MIDDLE,

OR THE END? WHAT IS THE MOST IMPORTANT **WORD** IN THE SENTENCE "**I LOVE YOU**"?

THE WORD **LOVE**? BUT **WHO** LOVES **WHOM**? IN THE LANGUAGE OF **MATHEMATICS**,

1 + 1 + 1 = 3. EACH SYMBOL IS NECESSARY. IN EFFECTIVE **COMMUNICATION**

EVERY WORD IS IMPORTANT. ONE MAY BE **EMPHASIZED** MORE THAN ANOTHER,

BUT EACH WORD IS **NECESSARY**, OR IT SHOULD BE EDITED OUT.

The Value of Empty Space

Remember that to communicate effectively you must say what you want to say; you must use the entire image area.

We know what the image area is, but let's examine the word *use*.

Look at the photograph below. Surely you can appreciate the value of "empty" space in this visual communication. Of course, the space is not really empty, even if it is *filled with nothing*. The relationship is drawn to read "a small car in a big world."

USING "EMPTY SPACE."
SALT FLATS, UTAH

STAREWAY TO HEAVEN

Once, as a teenager having done something of which my mother would disapprove, I tried to sneak upstairs, hoping to avoid her. However, this was not to be; she caught me at the bottom of the stairs and proceeded to stare at me, saying nothing. This struck me as her harshest reprimand.

Clearly my mother had learned to use empty space to communicate effectively.

ACTIVITY 4.4: LONELY CIRCLE IN RECTANGLE

1. Start with an empty rectangle. Tell the child to put a circle of any size he chooses into the rectangle so that the image communicates loneliness.

2. Critique the result. Any number of answers are correct here, but the best answer would seem to be a small circle overwhelmed by the rest of the empty space in the rectangle.

FILL IT WITH NOTHING

THE CONCEPT IS TO **CONTROL**

THE IMAGE **AREA**, BUT THIS

DOES NOT ALWAYS **MEAN**

FILLING IT WITH SOMETHING.

FILLING IT WITH **NOTHING**

CAN BE AN **EXTREMELY**

EFFECTIVE MEANS OF

COMMUNICATION!

Balance

Balance often describes an image that is in harmony, at equilibrium, within itself. This is another extremely subjective term; for our purposes, *balance* applies to an image that looks and feels good and communicates the intended message. Note in the circle and square graphic how the empty space balances the small circle. The areas occupied

---

ACTIVITY 4.5: BALANCING ACT

Try this for an understanding of balance.

1. Have the child stand on one foot.

2. Gently push his upper body to one side while he continues to balance on one foot.

3. Notice how his free leg goes out to compensate and keep him balanced.

Other examples of balance:

The moon traveling around the earth

The earth traveling around the sun

---

by the circle and the empty space are not equal, but they are in the correct proportions to communicate the intended message, loneliness. Thus, the proportions are correct, the image is balanced.

Actually, we have come back to relativity. You can only appreciate sound if there is silence; music uses the silence between the sounds to establish a rhythm. A good speaker (or an angry mom) uses the space between the words. A person who communicates well in two-dimensional imagery often uses empty space in the picture.

The key word is *uses*. In Chapter 3 when the image maker placed her subject directly in the middle of the picture she was not controlling the empty space. Rather, it was controlling her. The uncontrolled empty space affected her communication, conveying the opposite of what she wanted to say.

BASSAM, IVORY COAST

In dollars and cents (sense?), if the photograph costs you a dollar, you should be aware of how you spend every penny. It is entirely appropriate to spend some of the money on empty space, as long as you are aware of it. Otherwise, you are wasting your money, and your communication will be worth less (worthless!).

DISSECTING THE RECTANGLE

In this section we are going to become acquainted with some of the most common "rules" of good two-dimensional composition.

The Rule of Thirds

Dividing the picture area in thirds can be quite pleasing. Placing important elements on these dividing lines often works well.

DIVIDING THE FRAME INTO THIRDS.
MR. HIGGINS AND ALBERT, OREGON

The Greeks liked the way their temples looked when they built them using the Golden Section Principle, dividing a line in such a way that the relationship of the smaller part (AB) to the larger (BC) is the same as the relationship of the larger (BC) part to the whole (AC).

A_____B_____ _____C

This produces a ratio of approximately .63. This is nearly a division into thirds, which would be approximately .67.

A rectangle can also be aligned vertically and divided in thirds. Thus, important compositional areas exist

1. along the lines dividing the composition in thirds, as well as
2. at the points where these lines intersect.

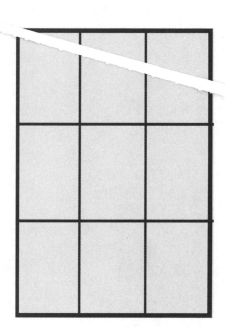

The Four Sides

We have already discussed the importance of the sides of the frame. They determine what is in and what is not in the picture. They are crucial not just because of the information they include, but also for what they *exclude*. Photography can be considered the "art of bold exclusion."

However, an image by no means ends at the frame. In the act of translating the image, the viewer often adds (extrapolates) action outside the frame to complete the image. Exactly how the image is cropped (where the sides begin and the picture ends) is critical in determining just how a viewer will put the image into context, imagining the action beyond the frame.

The direction of a subject's gaze creates a very strong force within an image. (For that matter, the same is true in the "real" world. Stare up at a building on a busy street and watch your fellow *homo sapiens* try to figure out what you're staring at.) For example, a person near the right side of the frame looking off to the right implies action outside the frame. Conversely, if the person on the right side is looking to the left, back into the picture, the viewer tends to resolve the meaning of the image within its frame.

ACTIVITY 4.6: ACTION OUTSIDE THE FRAME

1. Look at the photograph above. Ask the child to tell you what action he thinks is taking place immediately outside the frame of the photograph.

2. Now ask the child to make up a completely different scenario (scene) for the action outside the frame. It should be clear that context can be strongly implied by a particular image. However, action outside (as well as inside) the frame is open to individual interpretation.

"EXTRA" HEADROOM USUALLY
TRANSLATES INTO "SMALL SUBJECT."

The four sides also determine the amount of space within the photo. You can leave lots of space at the top (headroom) to indicate that the subject is small, or jam the subject up against the top of the frame to communicate "large."

The Corners

LITTLE OR NO HEADROOM INDICATES
A LARGE SUBJECT.

The sides of the frame are important, and the meeting of these sides at the corners is also important. Draw lines connecting the corners and you will find that they intersect directly in the middle of the frame. Important compositional areas exist along the lines connecting the corners, as well as at the intersections of these lines. (That's right, I admit it, the middle is important. I never said it wasn't.)

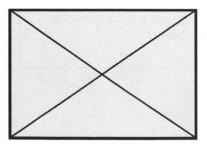

CONNECTING THE CORNERS

ACTIVITY 4.7: STRONG CORNERS

Have the child make an image in which the corners are visually important.

He can do this by making a photograph; selecting an image in a magazine and cropping into it to make another image that has dynamic corners; or using the Handy Cam.

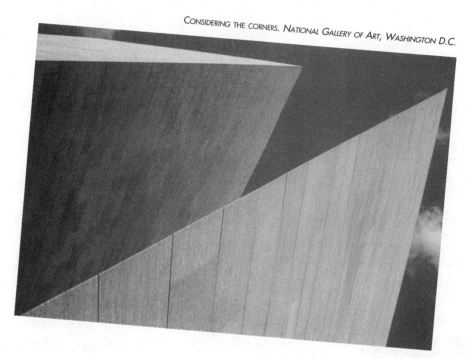

CONSIDERING THE CORNERS. NATIONAL GALLERY OF ART, WASHINGTON D.C.

Gravity

Our stereoscopic vision is arranged horizontally. Because *up* and *down* are big concepts for earthlings (just ask the *Sesame Street* characters), we factor gravity into our perceptions.

Perceptions of top and bottom enter into the manner in which we interpret images. Thus, when making images, the effects of gravity should be considered. How will the viewer resolve which direction is up and which is down? How is gravity at work in the image? Likewise, the relationship between the top and the bottom of the frame is important.

GRAVITY—AN IMPORTANT CONCEPT IN HUMAN PERCEPTION

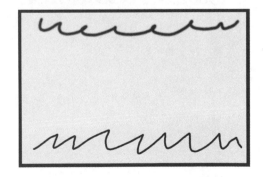

THE ENTIRE FRAME IS IMPORTANT.

THE WHOLE THING

To recap, the following are important elements in the composition of the picture area:

The division of the area in thirds
The four corners and the diagonals from them
The middle
The top and bottom
The four sides

In other words, *the whole thing is important,* the entire frame and exactly where that frame ends. Note that you need not actually know any of these rules. The key is simply to consider the entire rectangle and its effect upon the visual communication.

COMPOSING, ARRANGING THE ELEMENTS. *LDS HOSPITLAL, SALT LAKE CITY*

5 PORTRAITS

A **STRONG PORTRAIT** DOES NOT JUST SHOW US HOW A PERSON LO

IT ATTEMPTS TO GO **MUCH DEEPER** AND ACTUALLY TELL US

WHO THE PERSON IS.

---------------------→ **PEOPLE PICTURES**

Up until now the images we have been making and working with have been mostly unpeopled, without people. The reason, as previously discussed, has been to get the image maker to focus on the elements of communication—the grammar and syntax of visual literacy. The principle of good visual grammar, utilizing the entire image area, should be firmly established at this point. Now let's put people in our images.

ACTIVITY 5.1: FIRST PORTRAIT

1. The child should make a portrait of you or a friend using either the Handy Cam or a real camera. Of course, she should pay attention to the entire frame. Beware of a prevalent mistake—putting the subject's head directly in the middle of the frame. The head carries so much weight (the Mr. Potato Head syndrome) that the top half of the frame is left to fend for itself. Even if someone has learned to use the entire frame in her pictures without people, she will often still commit this common mistake—old habits die hard.

2. Critique the portrait. Is the entire frame being used?

A child will often make a poor first portrait, putting the person's head directly in the middle, thereby wasting the top half of the frame and cropping out some valuable information about the person.

When this happens I ask the photographer, "How did Chloe get in here anyway?" The child wonders about me, again, since she obviously walked in. I then point out, "But she doesn't have any feet," referring to the image with the feet cropped out. The point is made that the feet often can tell us a lot about a person. Certainly it would be more interesting to see the feet than the empty top of the frame.

USE IT OR LOSE IT!

HUMAN BEINGS **LEARN** BY

MAKING MISTAKES; THUS,

THE HIGHEST **GRADES** SHOULD

GO TO THE STUDENTS WHO **MAKE**

THE **MOST MISTAKES** AS LONG

AS THEY **USE** (PROCESS) THEM!

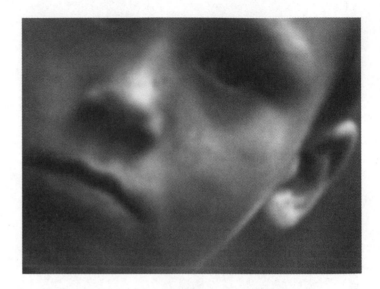

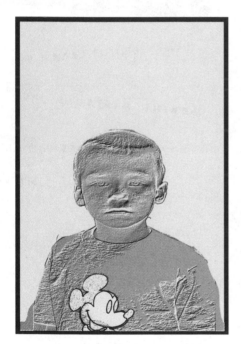

THE STRONG TENDENCY AND BAD VISUAL HABIT
OF CENTERING THE HEAD

MORE IMPORTANT THAN BOB

I once worked with a third-grade child who had learned to utilize the entire frame, but he fell back on bad habits when attempting a portrait of his classmate, Bob. He put Bob's head directly in the middle of the photo, wasting the top third of the image area.

When we critiqued his image, he realized his mistake. I sent him out to make another photo of Bob. This time he was so close that Bob was out of focus and one of his eyes was even cropped out. When I showed the class this photo, they all howled. It was a very successful image.

When I asked the child why the second picture was such a success even though parts of Bob were missing, he replied, "That's because the photograph is more important than Bob!" A brilliant answer, and of course correct.

When attempting to communicate a message (in this case, Bob), you must first and foremost pay attention to the mode of the communication. If you don't pay attention to what a photograph is—a two-dimensional language with its own rules of grammar—you will fail to communicate. Another way of putting it: You must first be aware of the reality of the situation, in this case a communication on a piece of paper, if you want to use it to any good end. Yes, the piece of paper, the photograph, is more important than Bob!

ACTIVITY 5.2: CHARACTER

1. Have the child choose a subject for another portrait. Ask her to list three important characteristics of the subject. These characteristics can be either "material" (tall, skinny) or "spiritual" (kind, smart) in nature.

2. Ask the child to design a portrait(s) of the person that will somehow communicate these characteristics. (The term *design* means that the child should plan the portrait and discuss her plan with you before she makes her image.) She can use either a photograph, the Handy Cam, or a drawing to make the portrait. Here's an example of a design plan:

Michael: 1. is a man; 2. is a painter; 3. loves his kids.

The photograph will illustrate what he looks like and what he does (numbers 1 and 2). It will also show that he brings his kids with him (number 3).

The design plan could also be a rough drawing of what the photograph will look like.

3. Critique the design with the child on two levels:

Grammar: Is the entire frame being utilized? Is the visual grammar good (foreground/background, corners, color)?

Content: How well is the message being communicated? Who is this person? Are the characteristics of the person clearly communicated? Would a stranger really know something about the subject from this portrait?

THE PAINTERS

THE KEYS TO STRONG IMAGES

WHEN AN IMAGE IS **GOOD**, WHEN IT IS A **STRONG** COMMUNICATION, IT ALWAYS WORKS ON **TWO LEVELS**. THE **CONTENT** OR MESSAGE IS **INTERESTING**, AND THE **VISUAL** GRAMMAR IS GOOD—IT IS **PRESENTED WELL**. **FUNCTION** AND **FORM** UNITE, THE MESSAGE IS **CLEAR** BECAUSE IT IS **PHRASED WELL**.

6

TIME:
THE FOURTH DIMENSION

WHEN YOU **LOOK** UP AT THE STARS, YOU ARE ACTUALLY LOOKING **FAR BACK** INTO THE

PAST. THE NEAREST **STAR** IS TWO LIGHT-YEARS AWAY, OR APPROXIMATELY

11,756,000,000,000 MILES. **TRAVELING** AT 186,000 MILES **PER SECOND**, IT TAKES

LIGHT TWO YEARS TO GO THAT DISTANCE. THE LIGHT YOU ARE **SEEING** LEFT THAT STAR

TWO YEARS AGO. SOME **STARS** ARE SO FAR AWAY THAT THEIR LIGHT HAS BEEN TRAVELING

FOR **THOUSANDS** OF YEARS TO REACH US. THE STAR YOU WISH UPON

MAY NO LONGER **EXIST** EVEN THOUGH YOU SEE ITS LIGHT!

THE RELATIONSHIP OF TIME TO VISUAL LITERACY

People who can communicate effectively using pictorial means are similar to people who can communicate effectively using the written word. The former represent the real world in pictures; the latter translate it into words. For these two-dimensional communications to be effective, the viewer or reader must be able to translate them readily into his own reality, which has four dimensions: height, width, depth, and time.

We have already discussed some of the grammatical devices used to communicate: foreground and background, overlapping elements, relative size, prior experience, and the use of the entire frame. But, we may not be all that familiar with time. Why is it the fourth dimension? Why must we consider it if we want to know what is real?

GOOD TIMING

BASKETBALL ARTISTS **LARRY BIRD** AND **MAGIC JOHNSON** WOULD NEVER **THROW**

THE BALL TO THE PLACE WHERE A TEAMMATE **WAS** AT A PARTICULAR **MOMENT**.

INSTEAD, THEY'D THROW TO WHERE HE'D **BE** IN THE **NEXT** SPLIT SECOND.

1. Tell the child that the sun is approximately 93,000,000 miles from us on Earth. Light travels at approximately 186,000 miles per second. (It could travel around the Earth more than seven times in one second! In fact, until the middle of the last century, scientists debated whether it had any speed at all. Many thought it was instantaneous.)

2. Work out with the child how long it takes the sun's light to reach us. (Get out the calculator and help the younger kids with this. It's a nice math exercise.)
Answer: 500 seconds.

How many minutes is this?
Answer: 8.33 minutes.

3. It takes the sun's light 8.33 minutes to reach us. Ask what would happen if the sun suddenly burned out and stopped producing light five minutes ago.

What would you see?
Answer: the sun, for another 3.33 minutes! Whenever you look at the sun you are looking back in time 8.33 minutes. Thus, you are seeing the sun, which burned out in our conceptual experiment five minutes ago, because you are seeing what it looked like 8.33 minutes ago when everything was fine.

4. Could you take a picture of this sun that no longer exists? Answer. Yes. You could even be tanned by it for another 3.33 minutes, even though it no longer exists in our activity. This is reality as we know it. To deal with reality, to know with accuracy where something really is, we must consider time.

It's true that in our everyday lives we need not always consider the speed of light; however, time has a tremendous impact on our lives:

Were you on time?
Did you get enough sleep?
Did you have enough time?
What time is it? here or in Paris?
Till death do us part
Life expectancy
Timing
A Good Time

THE STILL PHOTOGRAPH

When you make a photograph, in effect, you've removed the passage of time. You have recorded the light at a particular moment. You have frozen an instant of time (1/250th of a second is a common shutter speed). However, the passage of time is always implied, and the viewer adds a time element, since our reality *always* has a temporal component.

A MOMENT OF TIME EXTENDING ACROSS THE IMAGE: SHADOW OF THE FUTURE, FOOTPRINTS OF THE PAST. *SOUTHERN UTAH*

ACTIVITY 6.2: TIMING

Find some images in magazines or books that exemplify different types of implied time. Share these with the child.

Examples

Timeless: time not a major factor

Portraits such as the *Mona Lisa*

Action: the very idea of movement; action takes place over time

A sports action photograph

An Event: a happening of historical significance

The pope in New Orleans; Woodstock

A Moment: a significant point of time in a series of incidents; a scenario that has an implied past and present

A boy and girl kissing; two people angrily conversing

The actual passage of time can be rendered visually, usually by using a slow (more than 1/15th of a second) shutter speed. We read the blur as the passage of time, as action over a short period of time. It can add a "dimension" (time) to the image, producing a powerful effect.

THE JUGGLING SMITHS

THE USE OF BLUR TO INDICATE ACTION

A blurred photo can also result from camera movement or lack of steadiness. In low light conditions, the automatic camera chooses a slow shutter speed, which makes it very difficult to get a sharp photo unless you use a tripod to hold the camera steady. This type of image is generally regarded as a mistake, a communication failure. It differs greatly from an intentionally blurred image used to communicate the passage of time.

A C T I V I T Y   6 . 3 :   B L U R R Y

1. Here is a good illustration of how a photograph can be blurred by movement. Put chalk on the fingers and palm of your hand. Carefully place your hand with your fingers spread apart on a blackboard. Quickly remove your hand. A relatively clear hand print

should remain. You can also do this activity with fingerpaint on paper, or in the sand.

2. Now repeat this action, except this time move your hand in a circular fashion while it is in contact with the board. The image that

remains will be a blur, unrecognizable as a hand.

When light enters the camera it "draws" on the film. If the film (the camera) is moved while this drawing is being made, the image will be blurred.

FOCUS VS. BLUR: THE PASSAGE OF TIME PHOTOGRAPH

You may think that you are holding your camera steady; however, if the shutter speed is 1/30th of a second or slower, it is very difficult to make a sharp image while holding the camera by hand. Even the act of pushing the shutter button causes enough movement ("noise" in photographic jargon) to blur your photo if the shutter speed is a slow one.

At faster shutter speeds, the camera's shutter opens and closes so rapidly that light enters for only a split second, with time to "draw" only one image. (A blur is actually a number of continuous images of the same subject upon the film.)

At a shutter speed of 1/1000th of a second and faster, you can actually be waving the camera in your hand and the photo will not be blurred.

Focus

There is a point at which the light rays from an object, which bend as they pass through a lens, come together, or converge. This point must correspond exactly with the film plane in the camera or the retina of the eye, if the object is to be seen clearly, in focus. The lens is adjusted, focused, so that the light rays from objects at a specific distance from the camera will converge on the film. All objects at that distance will be in focus. (I almost said that they will be sharp, but they may be in focus and camera movement over time may cause them to be unsharp!)

Objects unintentionally out of focus can destroy the communication that the photographer desired. Unintentional blur can have the same negative effect upon the communication. However, if intentional, these effects can also be used to enhance the visual communication.

OTHER ASPECTS OF TIME IN PHOTOGRAPHY

Sequence

One way to use time in photography, or in any still image, is in a *sequence*, a number of images purposefully following one another in a set order.

THE SEQUENCE. *FIRST STEPS*

The combining of numerous two-dimensional images and sound, in rapid sequence, becomes film or video.

Series

A series of images is a group; however, one does not necessarily follow the other in real time. Rather, the photographer or artist puts the images together to communicate something. The images need not be of the same thing or even in the same medium.

THE SERIES. *WORKING WOMEN*

THE TIME IS RIGHT

TIMING IS A CRUCIAL ASPECT OF HUMAN COMMUNICATION. PAY ATTENTION TO THE MANNER IN WHICH THE FOURTH DIMENSION, TIME, IS REPRESENTED IN THE VISUAL IMAGE. IT'S THERE. TAKE THE TIME TO BECOME AWARE OF IT.

ACTIVITY 6.5: SERIES

1. Have the child assemble images from any number of sources and make a series that communicates something to the viewer. Try to make this first communication obvious and specific (love, litter).

2. Critique the series. A series is really an extended frame, a larger context than a singular image. But the same criteria apply: Is it all necessary? Does it all work? Are the elements placed most effectively?

MEANING

VIET NAM MEMORIAL,
WASHINGTON, D.C.

WHERE AM I?

GOOD ART IS OFTEN CHARACTERIZED AS INVITING YOU IN

THEN NOT LETTING YOU KNOW WHERE YOU ARE.

Rich Parks, administrative artist

THE PICTURE FRAME: INSIDE AND OUT

The message, the meaning, the communication derived (read) from any image involves the entire image area and all its internal relationships. It also involves all of the external relationships that the image evokes.

Internal Relationships

These include all of the elements within the frame and how they relate to each other:

Is the boy bigger than the building? (He's dominant, important.)

Or is the boy small in the frame? (He's fragile, unimportant.)

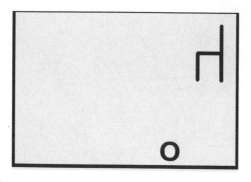

A BALL FELL OFF THE CHAIR?

ACTIVITY 7.1: ADD A CHAIR OVER THERE

1. In Activity 4.4 the child placed a small circle inside an empty rectangle to communicate loneliness. Now the child should add a chair to the picture.

2. Discuss the new meaning that the addition of the chair creates.

Again, there is no correct answer. The point is that given another element (a chair), the viewer will attempt to organize the information into some type of communication and give it some type of meaning.

Central Park West, New York City

CONTEXT

THE CONTEXT IS THE **LIFETIME** (SHORT OR LONG) OF **EXPERIENCES** THAT EACH **INDIVIDUAL** BRINGS TO THE SPECIFIC **MOMENT** OF **ENCOUNTERING**, LOOKING AT, A VISUAL **IMAGE**. EACH PERSON **READS** AN IMAGE FROM HER OWN **INDIVIDUAL** CONTEXT.

External Relationships

These arise from the correspondence between the elements in the frame and those outside the frame, in the world-at-large.

We know from our experience that buildings are large; therefore, if the boy appears larger than the building, he is very important, "larger than life."

If someone nearly drowned as a child, a beautiful image of the ocean may be terrifying to her.

Oregon Coast

WHAT DOES IT MEAN? ←————————————————————————

Meaning is the most important part of any discussion on communication. *What does it all mean?* It can also be the most difficult to come to terms with, since meaning is ultimately subjective. The person who created an image may have had in mind an entirely different communication, message, meaning, than the one that the viewer receives.

Therefore, for effective communication to take place, it is extremely important that both the image's creator and the image's viewer have a grasp of visual literacy. This is the ability to state your message clearly, to say what you mean visually. Visual literacy is also the ability to read the visual communications of another person, to understand what that person is attempting to say to you.

A FAILURE TO COMMUNICATE?

THE LARGE **BRAIN** THAT WE POSSESS AS *HOMO SAPIENS* SEEMS TO HAVE DEVELOPED SPECIFICALLY AS A **COMMUNICATION** TOOL WITH ADVANCED **LANGUAGE** POSSIBILITIES.

THOSE **CREATURES** WITH SIMILAR BRAINS—DOLPHINS AND WHALES—HAVE HIGHLY DEVELOPED **LANGUAGES** THAT WE HAVE NOT YET BEEN ABLE TO DECIPHER. OUR SUCCESS OR FAILURE AS A **SPECIES** WILL PROBABLY DEPEND UPON OUR ABILITY TO USE **LANGUAGE SKILLS** TO COMMUNICATE.

1. Have the child look at the photographs on this and the preceding page. Ask her to assign a one-word title to each image. She can either write these down, or you can write them down for her.

2. Discuss the titles. Explore the communications. Ask the child to put into words why she chose each particular title. How does a particular title change the meaning of an image? You may even ask the child to write an explanation for each title. Children who don't normally like to write will often write about their feelings in response to visual images.

ACTIVITY 7.3: FEELINGS

1. Have the child choose a "feeling" word: hot, tired, happy, and so on. *Laughter* would not be a feeling word. Rather, it is a physical reaction to a feeling. Try to keep this distinction in mind.

2. Ask the child to make an image (Handy Cam, drawing, photograph, magazine cutout) that communicates this feeling to the viewer without using people. If images of people were allowed, she might just take an image of someone experiencing a particular feeling. In this activity the child will have to work a little harder to find an image that communicates the particular feeling.

3. The child should tell you why she chose the image she did to communicate the feeling.

4. Critique the result. Does it work? Why? Why not? Could it be made better? How?

There are obviously no right or wrong answers here, but an opportunity to examine how the child reasons. This activity provides a chance to communicate with the child, to explore what and how she thinks and feels. You in turn can share your feelings with her. You can learn a lot here. Be aware. Have fun.

REALISTIC IMAGES

We have been dealing with images containing elements that we can identify. Even though the message may be conceptual, such as a feeling, the images have contained recognizable objects. We can call these images *realistic* in style. They have a direct link to something in the "real" (material) world.

Actually, we have used this strong photographic link to reality to learn that the photograph is a language representing a tree, but it is not in fact a tree. (Okay, I remember, I was corrected once already, it is on a slice of tree. Whose book is this anyway?!) Even the paintings of the Impressionists and Expressionists can be identified (a face, a bridge), although they are often far from "realistic."

ABSTRACT IMAGES ◄──────────────────────

For our purposes, we can think of abstract images simply as those that we cannot easily identify.

ABSTRACT IMAGE

AGREEING TO DISAGREE

"WHAT DOES IT MEAN?"

ALMOST ALWAYS IMPLIES

THE ADDITION OF THE PHRASE

"TO YOU." WHEN PEOPLE

CAN AGREE TO DISAGREE,

THEY CAN COMMUNICATE.

ACTIVITY 7.4: TITLING ABSTRACT IMAGES

1. Have the child look at the abstract image on the preceding page.

2. Ask the child to title the image.

3. Ask her to explain the title.

ACTIVITY 7.5: MAKING ABSTRACT IMAGES

1. Ask the child to start with a "feeling" word like love, anger, hope, and so on.

2. Having chosen a word, the child should now make an abstract image that in some way communicates this feeling, this idea. She can make the image by drawing, photographing (Handy Cam or real camera), or "finding"—taking a part of an image from a magazine or a newspaper.

3. The child should now explain why she chose this particular image to "illustrate" her feeling word. This is another great writing opportunity, but it must be "real" to the child, pleasurable, and fun.

8 COLOR

THE KEYS TO UNDERSTANDING COLOR

MR. SHARP WITH JASPER JOHNS'S UNITED STATES PAINTING,
MUSEUM OF MODERN ART, NEW YORK CITY

DO **YOU** LIKE IT?

WHAT DOES IT MEAN TO **YOU**?

HOW DOES IT AFFECT **YOU**?

PAY ATTENTION TO THE COLOR

Color (or the lack of it) is an important element in any visual image. Our brains translate the various wavelengths of the visible spectrum into colors. A basic understanding of color helps in the creation as well as the reading of visual images. It would be foolish to attempt to deal with color theory in any great depth in this black and white (shades of gray) book. However, I encourage you to delve further into color studies. The work of Josef Albers and Edwin Land as well as other color theorists is valid, important, and extremely interesting.

Here is a standard list of the characteristics of color:

Hue: the color, the name of the color, red through violet, as determined by the dominant wavelength
Value/Brightness: the relative darkness or lightness of a color; the darkness or lightness of a color if it were reduced to shades of gray
Saturation/Intensity: the purity or strength of a color; how much of its complement is or is not present in the color; the "redness," "blueness," and so forth of the color

The concept is quite simple: Pay attention to the color. All color studies and theories are based upon how *homo sapiens* respond to color, the wavelengths of energy that we can perceive as visible light, the visible spectrum. Therefore, you are your own best learning instrument. Follow your feelings when it comes to color.

A C T I V I T Y   8 . 1 :   T H E   N A T U R E   O F   C O L O R

1. Find an object with one dominant color (a red coat, a blue hat, and so forth). Ask the child what color this object would be if it were in a totally dark room (without any light). Of course, it couldn't be seen, but would it still be red, blue, or whatever?

2. The answer is no, it has no color in a totally dark room. The color of the object comes from the light that lands on it and the wavelengths that are reflected back off of it. When normal white light containing all the colors in the spectrum strikes a red object, the light's energy is converted into heat and absorbed, except for the red wavelengths which remain as light and are reflected off the object. The dyes used perform this function like a net or filter, absorbing some wavelengths and converting them into heat, and reflecting others. Different dyes or paints reflect different wavelengths and absorb others. Clearly, if no light falls on an object, it has no color. (Does a tree make a noise if it falls in the forest and no one is there to hear it? Clearly yes, since sound waves are created and humans are not the center of the universe. But that's another book.)

By the way, white reflects all the colors and they remain as light. Since all the colors together appear as white, the object is the color(s) white. Very little energy is absorbed as heat. Thus white clothes are cool, man. Black clothes are hot since almost all the light is converted to heat and none is reflected back as light. Black is the absence of light.

COMPLEMENTARY COLORS

A complementary color completes its complement. Here's a widely accepted theory of why this happens:

When you look at red, your optic system uses red receptors. When they are being used, they quickly become fatigued, and they want to shut down, to rest. If the red receptors rest, then the information sent to your brain is devoid of red, and you see a green image. Green is red's complement; think of the green receptors as the opposite of the red ones.

ACTIVITY 8.2: COMPLEMENTARY COLORS

1. Hold a piece of bright red construction paper up against a white wall.

2. Tell the child to stare at the red piece of paper and not to divert his eyes. Tell him you will be holding up the piece of paper for about forty-five seconds. Alert him to the fact that his eyes will probably feel some fatigue, but that he should do his best to stick with it.

Note: This activity works best if the paper contains a particularly sharp geometric shape (a square, a rectangle, a triangle, a star).

3. As the child stares at the red shape, tell him that soon you will be removing it and that when you do so, he should continue to look at the white wall. Tell him that he will probably see something on the white wall, and you will want to know the shape and color of what he sees.

4. After approximately forty-five seconds, quickly remove the red shape. Ask the child what color and shape he sees. His answer will probably be that he sees a green shape on the white wall in the identical shape, placement, and size as the red shape. When he

moves his head, the image will move on the wall.

5. Repeat the activity with a green shape (he will see red), a blue shape (he will see yellow), and a yellow shape (he will see blue).

6. Explain that each color has its complement. Note that this word is spelled with an *e* not an *i*. It is derived from the word *complete*, and is not related to the word *compliment* (nice hair).

When your eye looks at the red, it gets tired and wants to see green. Then, when you look at something green, you see the green with an afterimage of green over it, thus the green appears more green, "greener." The red makes the green appear more intense. Then, when your eye returns to the red after looking for a few seconds at green, the red appears even more red since you are now carrying an afterimage of red in your brain.

The way in which our eyes (bodies) see causes red and green to contrast with each other so as to make the other color appear more intense. The same effect takes place between complements like yellow and blue. All the other shades in between also have complementary opposites. It is important to note that the "rules of complementary colors" are contained *within your body*, not in any book, not even this one.

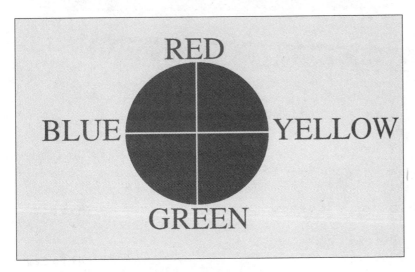

THE COLOR WHEEL: COMPLEMENTS ARE DIRECTLY OPPOSITE EACH OTHER.

ACTIVITY 8.3:
COMPLEMENT EACH OTHER

1. Ask the child to observe and list some common uses of complementary colors: Christmas, traffic lights (red and green), backpacks, ski jackets (blue and yellow).

2. Have the child make a photograph or drawing that utilizes complementary colors. He can also use his Handy Cam to find complementary pairs.

COMPLEMENTARY COLORS ACCENTUATE EACH OTHER.

COMPLEMENTS VS. NONCOMPLEMENTS

USING COLOR **EFFECTIVELY** IN NO WAY MEANS **ALWAYS** USING **COMPLEMENTS** TOGETHER. THE IMAGE MAKER MAY WISH TO **DOWNPLAY** THE DIFFERENCES OR **CONTRASTS** WITHIN AN IMAGE FOR A "**SOFTER**" EFFECT. THEN THE USE OF **DIRECT** COMPLEMENTS SHOULD BE AVOIDED. **BE AWARE** THAT EVEN IN THIS CASE THE **EFFECTS** OF **COMPLEMENTARY** (AND **NONCOMPLEMENTARY**) COLORS ARE BEING **USED**.

1. Ask the child to make an image that screams a certain color: red, green, blue, and so forth. (He can use his Handy Cam, a real camera, or a collage, but no drawings. He must find the color.) The image should be such that the very first thing that strikes the viewer about the image should be its color. The color should override in importance any subject matter. This may be easier to accomplish in an abstract image, but attempt to use a realistic one. Be sure that color is the primary subject matter.

2. Critique the result. Is the main communication the chosen color?

BLACK AND WHITE

Black and white are also complements; when you look at a black image, your mind sees a white afterimage and vice versa.

HIGH CONTRAST—FEW OR NO MIDTONES

CONTRAST

Contrast is the relationship between tones or shades of gray within an image. The photograph on page 119 is called a *high-contrast* photo because the tones are as far apart as the printing ink and the paper base will allow. There are no mid-ranges, only black and white. Occasionally an image like this can be found in nature. Backlit images often appear high in contrast. But, generally, a high-contrast image is created in the darkroom, on the computer, or in the printing process.

A low-contrast image has lots of tones that are close to each other, that are similar shades of gray. This image is usually devoid of any dark blacks or white whites.

LOW CONTRAST—NO BLACKS OR WHITES. *THE LOUVRE, PARIS*

FULL TONAL RANGE. *THE EPPERSONS*

ACTIVITY 8.5: TONE IN, TUNE IN

1. Turn your television's color down until you have a black-and-white TV, or use a black-and-white TV.

2. Find the contrast control knob and let the child play with it. Have him make the image high contrast. Then make it low contrast. Notice the differences.

3. Let the child set the contrast control for television viewing. Ask why he chose this setting. "It looks the best," is an appropriate answer.

4. Experiment with the brightness control on the television. Observe and discuss the difference between the contrast (separation of tones) and the brightness (overall light and dark) of an image.

5. Let the child set the brightness.

6. Finally, let the child bring the color back and choose the "best" color level. It is important that children (and adults) learn to control their television sets and not the other way around.

TRUST YOUR SENSES

THE KEY LESSON IS THAT THE "**RULES**" OF **COMPLEMENTARY COLORS** (AND INDEED, OF ALL **VISUAL LITERACY**) ARE CONTAINED **WITHIN YOUR OWN BODY**.

TRUST YOUR **SENSES** AND PAY ATTENTION TO THE WAY THEY **RESPOND** TO STIMULI AND THE OUTSIDE WORLD. ALMOST **EVERYTHING** CONTAINED IN THE LITERATURE ON VISUAL LEARNING AND VISUAL LITERACY IS **ACCESSIBLE** THROUGH YOUR OWN **HONEST EFFORT** COUPLED WITH **TRIAL AND ERROR** (INCLUDING ALL OF THE INFORMATION CONTAINED IN THIS **BOOK**, ALTHOUGH YOU HAVE **HOPEFULLY** ALREADY PAID FOR IT).

9 MEDIA LITERACY

THE ADVERTISER'S CREED

I **CANNOT** LIE, BUT I SURE CAN **IMPLY**.

FROM THE FILM PROMISED LAND, SALT FLATS, UTAH

READ THE FINE PRINT

Now you are ready to apply the lessons of visual literacy to the world of the media, most specifically to advertising communications (print and electronic) and to television itself. These practical applications will hopefully enable you and your child to make informed decisions about these communications, which are everywhere in daily life. And paying attention to these will also sharpen your visual literacy skills.

Reading the small print in an ad is the same as paying attention to the entire picture area. Why is it small? The advertiser is obliged to print it, but does not want you to pay attention to it. Read these visual and verbal signals; they will tell you a lot.

THE WORLD OF ADVERTISING

Think of it this way: The advertiser has a purpose behind her communication—to get you to buy the product. A cereal ad might imply that if you eat that cereal every morning, you will enjoy life more.

This is not to say that a certain product will not meet your particular needs. In most cases you can gather some very useful information about a product from its advertisement. Couple that with "the brain that God gave you" and you'll "have a nice day." THINK.

WORD POWER

ADVERTISE:

TO **DESCRIBE** A PRODUCT

IN SOME **MEDIUM**

IN ORDER TO **INDUCE**

THE **PUBLIC** TO BUY IT

TO INCREASE **SALES**

FIFTH AVENUE, NEW YORK CITY

ACTIVITY 9.1: I WANT IT

1. Have the child select an ad from a magazine. Ask her what specific product is being sold.

2. Ask what need or want the ad implies the product will satisfy. How is the ad appealing to the reader or viewer?

Be careful here. Don't ask what need the product *will* satisfy, but what need the ad *implies* that the product will satisfy. A soft drink ad may imply that the drink will enable you to have lots of fun and an instant party. It appeals to our desire to have fun; but the drink can really only satisfy your thirst, at best. In fact, the drink may contain ingredients that are actually harmful to your health; it may even make you more thirsty! An ad for a particular brand of coffee may show a sophisticated, beautiful, or handsome person enjoying the coffee at a very chic restaurant with very chic friends. The ad is communicating that if you drink this particular coffee, you will become sophisticated and rich.

3. How does the specific product link itself with this want or need? Consider the use of the entire advertising space and placement, size, distance, and color of the image(s).

4. What does the ad really tell you? What can you tell about the product from the ad? The answer will often be nothing. The information in the ad is incomplete (often purposefully), and it would be foolish to make any decisions based upon it.

Sometimes an ad provides lots of information, if you pay attention. If an ad is vague (using such phrases as "Up to 25% off"), you can be sure that the product is not as advertised.

THE PURSUIT OF HAPPINESS

THINK OF IT THIS WAY. THE

CONSUMER HAS A PURPOSE:

LIFE, LIBERTY, AND THE

PURSUIT OF HAPPINESS.

THE ADVERTISER'S PURPOSE IS

TO GET THE CONSUMER TO BUY

ITS PRODUCT. THE ADVERTISER

DOES THIS BY ASSOCIATING ITS

PRODUCT WITH THE SUCCESSFUL

PURSUIT OF HAPPINESS.

ACTIVITY 9.2:
MASSAGING THE MESSAGE

1. Find a print ad that combines words prominently with images, such as "No complaints" or "Just Do It."

2. What is the purpose of the communication? Ask the child:

What is the advertiser selling?

What message is being conveyed concerning your life, liberty, and pursuit of happiness? How does the ad appeal to your needs?

3. Dissect the ad with the child. Imagine the image(s) of the ad without the words. What do the image(s) alone communicate? What would the words communicate without the images? Be specific in your critiquing of the words. Consider what they actually say versus what they imply.

4. How do the words and images work together to communicate the advertiser's message? Treat this mixing of words and images as a single communication using two languages, the visual and the verbal (in this case, written). Remember how titles change the way images are understood.

Examine the use of space. Notice the way that the words and images are placed to interact with each other.

5. What does the ad really tell you? Can you tell anything about the product from the ad?

Charts and Graphs

Visual displays such as bar graphs can be used to mislead the viewer. Remember: Look carefully.

More than 98 percent of all Mammoth Trucks sold in the last ten years are still on the road.

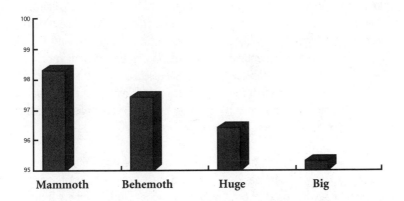

On the graph in this fictional Mammoth Truck ad, it appears that the advertiser's product is far superior to all of the competitors. However, if you look very closely, you will notice that the vertical axis indicates that the difference between Mammoth and Behemoth is actually less than one percentage point! And the difference between Mammoth and Big is actually only three percentage points, even though the visual makes Mammoth look five times better. The axis only plots points from 95% to 100%, not from 0% to 100%, as you might assume. The ad might be printed with an overlay, perhaps an exciting image of a truck plowing through the mud, to help divert the consumer's attention. Look sharp!

IN A TASTE TEST

THE PHRASE "PREFERRED IN A TASTE TEST" **MEANS** ABSOLUTELY **NOTHING**. IT'S POSSIBLE THAT THE **MANUFACTURER** ASKED ONLY **ONE** PERSON TO TEST THE **PRODUCT**, AND THAT PERSON WAS THE **PRODUCER'S** GRAND-MOTHER! OR, PERHAPS IN FIFTY TASTE TESTS THE ADVERTISER'S PRODUCT WAS CHOSEN **ONCE** AS THE BEST, AND A **COMPETITOR'S** PRODUCT WAS **CHOSEN** IN THE OTHER **FORTY-NINE**!

ACTIVITY 9.3: TELL IT LIKE IT ISN'T

1. Ask the child to decide on a message to communicate or a product to advertise. Remember that, in the spirit of advertising, the message need not be entirely true. Also, she doesn't have to choose an object to sell.

Second Avenue Is the Greatest Street to Live On

Ms. Brown Is the World's Best Teacher

2. Have the child list the strengths of the product, the really good things about it.

Pretty street, friendly people

Ms. Brown takes us on lots of field trips

3. Now list the weaknesses of the product, its downside.

Heavy traffic

She makes you work hard.

Notice that the "weaknesses" are relative. Ms. Brown makes you work hard, but this is probably a good thing. However, depending upon your intended audience, it may not "play" well. It might run counter to their interpretations of the pursuit of happiness.

4. The child should define the audience. Exactly whom does she want to buy her product or message?

Young married people

Fifth graders who have a choice of teachers

5. Ask the child to design a one-page ad selling her product or message.

She should use words and images to highlight the good things and downplay the bad. The child can draw a rough sketch, cut pictures out of magazines, or make actual photos. Don't judge drawing skills; achieving an understanding of communication and mixing media is the goal. Remember the advertiser's code: "I cannot lie, but I sure can imply."

6. Critique the ad. Is the space used well? How well do the words and images work together? Is the ad effective—will it persuade the target audience to "buy" the product? What could be changed to make the ad more effective?

TORREY, UTAH

COME TO QUAIL HOLLOW

While working with a sixth-grade class at Quail Hollow Elementary, I gave the following assignment: Design an ad to persuade fifth graders to come to sixth grade at your school. This assumed that fifth graders had absolute power to decide where to attend sixth grade.

Two boys created an ad with a photo of some pretty sixth-grade girls sitting on the playground equipment. Under the photo were the words

> COME TO QUAIL HOLLOW,
> WE HAVE HOT GIRLS

Sixth grade!? It surprised me too.

I pointed out that they had actually excluded half their possible audience by designing an ad that appealed only to boys. (It might appeal to a few girls, although I hope that most girls wouldn't buy into this kind of "objectification.")

On the other hand, two girls designed an ad that featured a photo of a forlorn girl sitting alone on the curb. Next to this photo was another of the girl with hands reaching down to help her up. She is smiling in this picture. Under the photos the caption read

> AT QUAIL HOLLOW WE
> INCLUDE EVERYONE

This ad appealed to every child's (person's) concern with being accepted, an important issue with fifth-grade boys and girls. Nice job, girls.

NOTHING UP THIS SLEEVE . . .

THERE ARE **TWO KEYS** TO

BEING A GOOD **MAGICIAN**:

1. CREATE A VISUAL **DIVERSION**

AT **JUST THE RIGHT** MOMENT.

2. PLAY UPON THE **PREJUDICES**,

THE **PRECONCEIVED** IDEAS,

OF THE **AUDIENCE**.

CONTEXT

ADVERTISING USES THE LANGUAGE OF WORDS TO PROVIDE **CONTEXT** AND CREATE

RELATIONSHIPS IN THE SAME WAY THAT IT USES THE VISUAL LANGUAGE. WHEN A TV AD

ANNOUNCES THAT A PRODUCT COSTS "**ONLY** $29.95," THE ADVERTISER IS **BUILDING** AN

ENVIRONMENT, A **CONTEXT**, THAT MAKES $29.95 SEEM **CHEAP**. AFTER MORE THAN

FOUR MINUTES OF **COMMERCIALS** DURING A RECENT SATURDAY MORNING CARTOON

SHOW, THE SMURFS RETURNED AND ANNOUNCED TO THE YOUNG AUDIENCE:

"**WE'RE BACK ALREADY**!"

Advertising Language

It is interesting to examine the way that language is used in advertising. Advertisers are generally restricted by law to "telling the truth." This means that their use of the language must not constitute a direct falsehood. However, advertisers often use the consumer's prejudices—preconceived ideas, wants, or wishes—to strengthen their sales pitches.

We saw a visual example of this with the bar graph on page 127. The hype around the ad—pictures of exciting Mammoth Trucks, boldface type claiming superiority—is designed to keep the consumer from looking closely at the coordinates on the bar graph. We assume that the coordinates are 0% to 100%; otherwise what's the big deal if all the manufacturers' trucks are within three percentage points of one another? (Any number of reasons could account for a small difference such as this. Perhaps Mammoth Truck owners spend so much money on repairs that they can't afford to get rid of their trucks!)

One way advertisers use the English language to their advantage is in their choice of articles: *the* or *a* and *an*. Remember:

> *The* is a definite article.
> *A* and *an* are indefinite articles.

If an advertiser has something good, and truthful, to say about a product, definite articles will abound to convey a definite message. When an advertiser is fudging the truth, then indefinite articles, *a* and *an*, serve the purpose well. Recognizing the advertiser's ambiguity will help you make good buying decisions. Remember, "in a taste test" tells you nothing.

DEFINITE

EXPLICITLY PRECISE

THE ART OF ADVERTISING

ADVERTISING IS THE ACT OF **INFORMING** YOU ABOUT A PARTICULAR PRODUCT, WITH THE **PURPOSE** OF GETTING YOU TO BUY IT. IF THE PRODUCT IS A GOOD ONE, IF IT SERVES YOU WELL AND HELPS MEET YOUR "**NEEDS**," THEN THE ADVERTISER NEED ONLY TELL YOU ABOUT THE PRODUCT **EFFECTIVELY**. IF, ON THE OTHER HAND, THE PRODUCT REALLY HAS **NO PURPOSE** IN YOUR LIFE, THEN THE ADVERTISER MUST CREATE A "**NEED**" IN YOU. MORAL: **BEWARE** OF **CREATED NEEDS**.

TELEVISION AND FILMS: ELECTRONIC IMAGES

Television is a fantastic medium, and when it is done well, it can enlighten and change our lives. Some of the best teachers I know use television extensively in their classrooms. However, in most cases TV shows are designed to deactivate you, keeping you interested on a passive level only. This, of course, is all a set-up for the punchline—the advertisements, which are usually the most visually interesting part of the entire experience.

CHROMA-KEY. THE TV WEATHERMAN EXCITEDLY POINTS AT NOTHING. TO VIEWERS, THE BLANK BLUE SCREEN IS FILLED WITH THE WEATHER MAP. ACTUALLY, ANYTHING BLUE WOULD PICK UP THE MAP. IF THE WEATHERMAN WORE A BLUE TIE, IT WOULD HAVE THE MAP ON IT! *MARK EUBANK, SALT LAKE CITY*

Television and film can be thought of as three-dimensional media—the two dimensions of the flat picture plane combined with the added dimension of time. Images move through space over periods of time, thus the term *moving pictures*. Sound also plays an important part, whether in the form of words, music, or noise. The active "viewer" must pay attention to this added dimension.

Watching television programs and movies intelligently requires you to employ the same critical perspective that you have been applying to still images and the world around you. Much of what is produced for television and the movies is intentionally made so that the viewer can drop in and drop out (tune in and drop out?). Paying constant attention is not required. This is not a haphazard occurrence. It follows a formula, the primary aim of which is to make money, not enlighten or inform.

Watching TV actively and developing active viewing skills makes a critical TV viewer. A critical TV viewer will use the television, be stimulated by it, and control its effect upon her life. Such a viewer will also be bored by bad TV and make the active choice to turn the television off when it is not meeting expectations.

SOUND UNHEARD

WATCH A TV SHOW WITH THE SOUND **TURNED OFF**. IS IT STILL **INTERESTING**? IF NOT, THEN TURN IT **OFF** COMPLETELY!

CONGRESSMAN WAYNE OWENS, WASHINGTON, D.C., 1989

1. Actively watch TV with the child. Focus on the ads. If you have a VCR, tape some ads. This will enable you to watch them a few times and refer to specific moments in the ads.

2. Critically review the ads. Have the child apply the same criteria to television ads that she applied to print ads. What is the purpose of the ads? What are they selling and to whom?

3. What particular need of the viewer does the ad play upon?

the need to be beautiful

the need to be accepted, popular

a physical need, such as a remedy for a medical condition

4. Have the child consider whether this "need" actually has anything to do with the product.

Jeans won't make you popular.

Beer won't make you beautiful.

Bran may make you regular.

5. Turn off the sound. How are the images, the visuals, used to convey the message that this particular "need" will be met? Encourage the child to use all of her visual literacy skills. Examine the link that the visuals "draw" between the viewer's "need" and the product.

Is the product colorful and large?

Are the people who are using it having fun, and are they "beautiful" people?

Conversely, if a comparison is drawn between products, how is the user of the competitor's product characterized?

6. What words does the ad use to convey that the product will meet the viewer's "need"? Are they spoken, written, or a part of the imagery? Look for prejudicing

words: "*Only* $29.95; *just* four payments."

7. How are sound and music used to get the message across to the target audience?

"Sophisticated" music: a "town" car

Blaring rock and roll: high-energy sneakers

Have the child imagine a completely different soundtrack (cheerful music during a scary scene). How would that change the effect?

8. How do the images, words, and sounds come together in the ad? Is the result effective, persuasive? If the child were an advertising person (and we all are, we all have a message to get across, we're human beings—communicative animals), what would she do to make the ad more effective? How would she change the images, words, and sounds?

Programming, Part I: Are They Just in It for the Money?

Commercial television sometimes offers good programs, but it's a show-by-show call. Do this reality check: Ask yourself why the program was made. Was it made to enlighten and entertain, using the entire space and time available to do so? Or was it made primarily to make money, as a set-up for the commercials? If the latter is true, then undoubtedly compromises were made in the quality. Most of these compromises will surface as a lack of attention to detail.

This is not to say that the wise allocation of resources does not have a place in television. No great project is ever completed without a great producer. The point is simple: What is the first and foremost motivating factor? Is it to communicate, or is it to make money?

WATCH WORDS

THERE IS NOTHING **WRONG**

WITH **TELEVISION**,

ONLY WHAT'S **ON** IT.

ACTIVITY 9.5: COMPARISON SHOPPING

1. Watch a commercial TV news program with the child (or a commercial TV cartoon); then watch a public TV news program (or a PBS children's program).

2. Compare with the child the commercial and public broadcast programs.

Which was more interesting? How and why?

Which was more entertaining? How and why?

Which was "better"? How and why?

What part did commercials play in the viewing experience?

Were the interruptions good or bad?

Programming, Part II:
The Quality of What We Watch

When critiquing television or film, consider whether the "entire space" is being used. You can usually tell when it's not; the product is boring and predictable. For example, an action film with great special effects will not be very entertaining unless the message and the manner in which it is delivered are interesting. Using the entire space, in this case, means that the film should communicate well on all levels—visual, verbal, and story (action). Many films today fall short because no real effort is made to tell the story well, or the story is a formula piece guaranteed to make money.

The most interesting TV shows and films require "active" participation on the part of the viewer. Subplots and character development encourage the audience to think. Also, the visual imagery is "interactive": The viewer who makes the effort can appreciate the angles, the colors, and the composition employed by the show's director. Sometimes the viewer must make choices within the frame, such as whether to focus on foreground or background action. The entire rectangular screen has been considered and used.

If you the viewer look for this level of quality on TV, and it's not there, then turn off the show. As soon as the child realizes that the POWER OFF switch is just as important, if not more so, than the POWER ON switch, the better off she will be.

QUALITY ENTERTAINMENT

THE AMOUNT OF **FUN**

INVOLVED IN BEING

VISUALLY **STIMULATED**

WHILE **ALSO** BEING

INTELLECTUALLY **CHALLENGED**

GUARANTEE

ASSURANCE OF

A PARTICULAR **OUTCOME**

ACTIVITY 9.6: START MAKING SENSE

1. The child should choose a TV show, film, or better yet, a music video of which she is particularly fond.

2. Have her view and describe in detail the first thirty to forty-five seconds. This description should note each time that there is a cut, a piece of action that is not continuous. She should note each cut, even in the same scene, within the same action. There may be dozens of cuts in thirty seconds of film. The cuts may be very subtle, or may constitute an entire change of scene.

3. Have the child dictate to you or write down the cuts herself. These descriptions are the beginning of what is called a *storyboard*. It includes a visual outline of each shot (cut): its length, the angle of view, close-up or distant, and the limits of the frame. It also details the sound effects, music, and dialogue, if any. Professional storyboards are often drawn on illustration board using frames in the shape of TV screens.

4. Help the child fill in her list of cuts with all the other elements of a storyboard. She will be amazed at how many different camera angles and cuts fill such a short period of time. Be very specific; note every change.

Here are some things to look for:

Changes in camera angle, point of view (POV)

Camera shots and angles:
- Looking up
- Looking down
- Eye level
- Close-up, medium range, or distant shot
- Stationary or moving camera position
- Zoom—camera moves in or out from the subject
- Pan—camera pivots to follow the action, or show another part of the scene
- Tracking Shot—camera moves to follow a subject

5. Go over the child's description (storyboard) with her. Discuss and critique why she thinks each move, each change, was made.

What was the purpose of each change?

Did it help tell the story?

How did each change contribute to the overall message, the concept, the communication of the piece?

6. Note with the child how much is entailed in making and controlling even thirty seconds of TV or film time. Notice also how our brains adapt to each move, perceiving the show as a seamless whole.

THE **OPENING SHOT** OF ROBERT ALTMAN'S **FILM** *THE PLAYER* RUNS **SEAMLESSLY**, WITH

NO CUTS, FOR **FIVE MINUTES**. IN THE SHOT, ONE OF THE CHARACTERS TELLS

ANOTHER HOW A **SHOT** IN THE FILM *THE BICYCLE THIEF* **LASTED**

SIX MINUTES **WITHOUT** A CUT. THIS IS A GREAT EXAMPLE OF

MULTIPLE LEVELS OF **ACTIVITY** AND **MEANING** TO **CHALLENGE** THE VIEWER.

INTERSTATE 80, FROM THE MOVIE PROMISED LAND

MAKING THE MEDIA LITERATE:
ROBERT REDFORD'S SUNDANCE INSTITUTE,
DEDICATED TO THE DEVELOPMENT OF
QUALITY INDEPENDENT FILMS, SUNDANCE, UTAH

ISOLATION: ALONE IN ← ─────────────────────→
A VAST WASTELAND

The danger for the viewer (and for our society, since the average person watches five hours of TV a day) lies in becoming desensitized. The medium acts as a depressant. Simultaneously bored and seduced by its sounds and colors, the viewer can no longer critically evaluate the medium or the message. (I knew someplace in this book I would use *medium* and *message* in the same sentence; words made famous by the late, great Canadian media criticism guru, Marshall McLuhan.)

This is especially dangerous because, for most people, TV viewing is a solo experience. Even when the whole family watches, there tends to be little or no interaction among the viewers. Diana, a friend of mine, does not have a TV. She told me that her ten- and twelve-year-old boys recently came home from a friend's house where the family was watching TV. The boys couldn't get over the way that the family sat facing the television, everyone staring. Their very body language indicated of a lack of interaction.

The critical viewer often feels alone in protesting the quality of television. After all, if millions find this entertaining, it must be so. The isolation of the viewer is a major reason that commercial TV can get away with programming of questionable quality. Denigration of the individual characterizes any mass dehumanizing experience.

CONSTRUCTION WORKER OR ACTOR?

DECONSTRUCTION WORKER

One winter's day I popped a video into the VCR in a fourth-grade class. The students asked, "What are we going to watch, John?"

"We are not going to watch; we are going to de-construct," I replied.

I showed them a thirty-second TV ad for a cold remedy. A hard-hatted construction worker slogs through puddles on a cold, dismal day at a muddy construction site. His lines: "It ain't right to let these boys down. I have to be here every day no matter how I feel. It don't cut me no slack."

We viewed it once, then I asked my first question: "What does this man do for a living?"

Hands shot up. "He's a construction worker!" Their teacher nodded approvingly. I hung my head.

Noticing my demeanor, one child came to the rescue. "He's not a construction worker, he's an actor!" Bravo.

Next I turned the TV around so that they couldn't see the picture and I played the commercial again. They paid attention to the sound. "He talks dumb," one student observed.

"Why?"

"Because construction workers are dumb," he replied.

"Does anyone's dad or mom work in construction?" Three hands went up. "Are they dumb?" I asked. Of course the answers were no, no, and no!

I continued, "Well then, why do they have this actor, playing a construction worker, acting dumb?"

"Because construction workers are dumb," a boy insisted.

"That doesn't seem right," I countered. "The only three construction workers that we have experience with in this class are all smart!"

From there we launched into a discussion of stereotypes and an examination of our prejudices.

Then we returned to the video. This time I played it without sound so the kids could pay attention to the images. The ad was filmed in a "documentary style," a herky-jerky frame with people stepping in between the camera and the "construction worker."

At one point I froze the frame. It contained a close-up shot of the worker at a point when he was so far to the right of the frame that half of his face was cropped out of the picture. The rest of the frame was empty. "This photographer sure did a lousy job. Look at the way he messed up on this shot! Oh, by the way, commercial photographers get paid about $2,000 a day!" I asserted.

"He meant to do it," one of the students exclaimed. "Why?"

"Because," she continued, "then we get the feeling that it was real. As though the photographer was chasing this construction worker around at the job." Bravo again.

"And what about the people getting in the way of the camera? Couldn't they get somebody to keep them out of the way?" I asked.

"They're there on purpose." Now the whole class was with it. "Yeah, it's all done on purpose!"

Those kids will never watch TV the same way again. The bottom line: "Yeah, it's all done on purpose."

STEREOTYPE

AN **OVERSIMPLIFIED**

PERCEPTION

OR **OPINION**

ACTIVITY 9.7: MY TURN

1. Have the child storyboard the opening minute or two of her own TV show or movie. Or, she can take a favorite song and storyboard a music video for it.

There are no budget constraints or technical limitations on the piece—the storyboard can be fanciful and fantastic, or not. It's her story.

2. Critique the storyboard with the child.

3. If you have a VHS or 8mm Camcorder available, help the child "film" the storyboard. If none is available, then let her "pretend" to make her film. Go through the entire process, set up the shots, rehearse and revise—do all except the actual filming. It's great fun.

If you are working with more than one child, this is a natural team activity. Most movies have huge crews. Teamwork is extremely important to good movie making.

4. This first film should be "short and sweet," thirty to sixty seconds maximum. Don't attempt to make *Ben Hur*, as it will only lead to discouragement. Besides, those chariot scenes are a mess to clean up after.

5. Critique the rehearsal and make whatever changes are necessary. Do one more revised rehearsal.

6. "Action!" If you are working without a Camcorder, stage the film and have the child show you her camera angles and describe her shots (close-up, wide-angle, zoom, pan, tracking). If you do have access to a Camcorder, then have the child "film" her short movie.

7. Critique the child's film, avoiding comparisons with professional productions. This first piece of filmmaking is not going to be slick. Emphasize the positive aspects and concentrate on the use of the

frame in your critique. Use the "still" or "pause" button to critique the use of the frame. Did the child practice the rules of good visual composition? Did she consider the entire frame and the relationships within it? How well has she communicated the message or story?

8. Discuss with the child the changes that might be made to improve her movie. It is beyond the scope of this book to explore adequately the possibilities in editing film. However, you can discuss and consider the following: reordering shots, lengthening or shortening the time of a particular shot, removing or adding footage.

9. Obtain funding ($20 million is the cost of the average feature) and let the child direct her story. (You can skip this step if you wish.)

10 THE ROLE OF THE COMPUTER

DESIGNING THE FUTURE

THE **APPEARANCE** OF A BUSINESS OR PERSONAL LETTER OFTEN HAS AS MUCH IMPACT UPON THE MESSAGE IT CARRIES AS THE WORDS THEMSELVES. THE **ARRANGEMENT** OF

HEADINGS AND PARAGRAPHS, THE **TYPE SIZE** AND FONT (TYPEFACE), AND THE AMOUNT OF EMPTY **SPACE** ALL PLAY IMPORTANT PARTS IN THE "**READABILITY**" OF THE LETTER. **PAY ATTENTION** TO THE VISUAL **DETAILS**—YOUR **COMPUTER** WILL DO AS IT'S TOLD (**USUALLY**).

COMPUTER LITERACY

In the last decade the personal computer has changed the way we process words. The latest technological advances, which promise to be even more dynamic, are changing the way we process images. Personal computers can now create images as well as scan existing images into their systems. These images can then be radically changed or modified.

The widespread use of the scanner will alter the way that we use the computer to communicate with each other. A scanner looks somewhat like a small copy machine. There are film scanners as well as hand-held models. When an image (a photograph, a drawing, or any graphic) is scanned into the computer, the image is digitized—converted into 0s and 1s (turns current on or off), the language that the computer uses to communicate with itself (talk to itself?!). Once this image has been translated—digitized—almost anything can be done with the computer to "rearrange the information."

The photo compact disc is another new technology that provides easy access to images for the computer. In addition, video boards and low-cost digitizers can digitize and store virtually any video, TV, VCR, and/or Camcorder image to use and reuse.

The activities in this chapter assume that you have very basic computer skills: turning it on and off, opening a program, and clicking the mouse. If you have access to a computer but have never tried it, this is your chance. Learn together with the child.

This activity will familiarize the child with the computer screen as a two-dimensional design tool. Letters will be used as design elements to blur the lines between words and images.

1. Open up any word processing application or drawing program.

2. Ask the child to type a letter of the alphabet. Use the mouse to highlight that letter. From the font menu, choose a type size 24-point or larger.

3. Ask the child to use the keyboard or the mouse to place the letter anywhere on the screen (the open page).

4. Evaluate how the letter looks sitting there by itself.

5. Type the same letter again and place it somewhere on the screen. How does it work with the first letter? How does the page look? Is it "pleasing"?

6. Do this three more times until you have a total of five letters on the screen.

7. With the child, critique the relationships between the letters, the design of the screen. Do they look good? Does the screen communicate any particular feeling to you?

8. Have the child rearrange the five letters. How does the screen look and feel now?

9. Try substituting any other letter or character. What happens to the look and feel of the screen when you use question marks or exclamation points? How about if you use numbers?

The computer screen, and of course its output, are visual representations (except when the printout is in Braille). Treat them as such. Certainly the symbols in our alphabet can be "arranged" to produce additional levels of meaning in the form of words. But, don't lose touch with reality; these symbols are contained within the context of visual information, the interpretation of which can be quite broad.

Dear Gramps,

Thanks so much for taking me to the museum.

I love you so much.

You are my Gramps.

Love,

Chloe

Dear Gramps,

Thanks *so* much for taking me to the museum.

I Love You So Much.

You are my Gramps.

Love,

Chloe

ACTIVITY 10.2: THE VISUAL LETTER

1. Ask the child to write a one-page letter. It might as well be a real letter to someone; keep the exercise interesting by sending it when it's finished. Include appropriate headings, margins, and salutations. Help young children write their letters.

2. With the child, evaluate, design, and redesign the letter, until it "looks" good. Change fonts, font sizes, margins, spacing, justification, and indentations. Experiment with drop caps and whatever other graphic capabilities your word-processing program possesses.

The best possible design maximizes the content of the communication. Play with all the different design possibilities. However, beware of using design elements just because they are available. All of the design choices should be made to enhance the letter's "message." The purpose of the design is to complement the meaning contained in the words.

If you have access to any drawing programs, or even a scanner and *Adobe Photoshop*, let the child become familiar with their capabilities. Use them early and often. As he learns how to talk to it, the computer will become a tool that can vastly increase the range and depth of his communications.

USING THE COMPUTER TO "MOVE" THE IMAGE'S INFORMATION FOR A PAINTERLY QUALITY. *2ND AVENUE*

LEARNING TOOL

BRYANT ELEMENTARY SCHOOL IN SAN FRANCISCO USES **COMPUTERS** EFFECTIVELY TO **INDIVIDUALIZE** THE LEARNING **PROCESS**. THE STUDENT'S **OWN IMAGE** GREETS HIM ON THE COMPUTER SCREEN WHEN HE OPENS **HIS** FILE. THROUGH **NETWORKING** CAPABILITIES STUDENTS FREELY, AND PROUDLY, **SHARE THEIR WORK** SCHOOLWIDE IN A **COMMUNITY** OF **LEARNING**. THE **KEY** INGREDIENT? THE COMPUTER SPECIALIST IS AN **EDUCATOR**, NOT A **TECHNOCRAT**.

Computers are powerful communication tools. At the advent of the computer age, they were often viewed as the embodiment of an increasingly dehumanizing social system. However, the personal computer has turned out to be the antithesis of the "every person is a number" doctrine. Especially now with the development of imaging capabilities, the individual can compete with, and to an extent resist, the powers in society that have heretofore almost exclusively controlled the mixing of words and images.

COMBINING AND MANIPULATING IMAGES

11 THE PORTFOLIO: A PERSONAL HISTORY

Joan Peterson, an enlightened educator from California, put it to me this way:

"**PORTFOLIOS** TELL US WHAT A CHILD **DOES** KNOW.

MOST **TESTING** TELLS US WHAT A CHILD **DOESN'T** KNOW."

AN INTERACTIVE RECORD OF ACHIEVEMENT

Using tests alone to assess a student's learning is unfair to both the student who tests well and the one who doesn't. Certainly if a student gets straight *A*s, we can assume that she has mastered the tested material; but she may actually know much more. The student who does not test well may know the material but approach it in a completely different way. She may also simply not be in sync with the particular testing process that was used.

Conversely, a portfolio can be significant in the life of a child. The development of a good portfolio is not a passive activity simply designed to help someone "evaluate" the child after the fact. Rather, it is a dynamic process that results in a living document. It can motivate and inspire a child to express herself and develop her creative potentials. Along with the attainment of new skills comes an increased sense of self-worth and self-esteem.

PARENTS TAKE NOTE

THIS SECTION IS NOT JUST FOR **TEACHERS**. (BESIDES, YOU CERTAINLY QUALIFY AS A **TEACHER**—THE MOST **IMPORTANT** YOUR CHILD **WILL EVER HAVE**!)

YOU ARE THE ORIGINAL **PORTFOLIO** MAKERS. CALL THEM BABY BOOKS, HOME MOVIES, MEMORY BOXES, WHATEVER YOU LIKE, **THESE** ARE THE THINGS OF WHICH PORTFOLIOS ARE **MADE**.

PORTFOLIOS: RECORDS OF ACHIEVEMENT. *ANASAZI RUINS, UTAH*

Portfolios can be, quite literally, our records of achievement. The British school system mandates that teachers develop a portfolio for each of their students in order to have some material, other than grades alone, that records the accomplishments of the child. They call these Records of Achievement. They are, quite literally, a visual celebration of each child.

Portfolios and Records of Achievement certainly broaden the scope of assessment. Most portfolios tend to have a visual component; if they don't, they generally suffer. In this section I will present some ideas that will help you develop a child's portfolio. Apply what you have learned so far about communication and visual literacy, and your attempts at portfolio building will be successful, rewarding, and fun.

HONOR THY CHILD

THE **PORTFOLIO** IS,

AND SHOULD BE,

A TREMENDOUS **OPPORTUNITY**

TO **HONOR**, TO PAY HOMAGE

IF YOU WILL, TO THE **HUMAN**

SPIRIT EMBODIED IN A

PARTICULAR **CHILD**. IT SHOULD BE

TREATED AS **NO LESS**.

Everyone agrees that the world would be a better place if there were more evidence of love and less of hate. The love that is most lacking is self-love, and this often manifests itself as hatred toward others. The term used is *self-esteem*, the respect one has for one's self. The concept is certainly in vogue, as it should be, and numerous programs aim at improving children's self-esteem. These efforts go for naught, however, unless a child feels worthy of her own respect because of the actual things she does, what she knows, and who she is.

Think of the portfolio as a way to communicate what a particular child does, what she knows, where she's been—WHO SHE IS.

Who is the audience for this communication? Anyone who ever looks at the portfolio for any reason at all. Certainly the teacher (or parent) who is helping to compile the portfolio. Finally, and most importantly, the child herself who is "recorded" in the portfolio.

The creation of the portfolio is a wonderful way to develop the child's skills. And, the portfolio also functions as a continual reminder to the child that there are many reasons why she should respect herself.

DEVELOPING A PORTFOLIO ←

As in any form of clear communication, a good portfolio will pay attention to everything that it is composed of: the visuals, the words, the sounds, if any, and how they come together.

A strong portfolio contains
1. Samples of the child's work, finished products
2. Documentation of the child's process, how the work came into being

KISS

KEEP IT SIMPLE, STUDENTS—

WORDS TO LIVE BY.

The Packaging

If you teach in a school district that mandates or provides a certain portfolio packaging, concentrate on individualizing the insides. If you are a parent or teacher who is free to decide on the portfolio's outside appearance, consider functionality. Choose a portfolio that will hold the necessary materials yet be extremely portable and easy to store and access. The substance will be on the inside; a nice monochrome cover with the child's name on it works just fine on the outside.

The Visuals

The visual portion of the portfolio can include the original work itself with the appropriate captions or explanations, always dated. Photographs are the best way to document when the original is not available (too large, a performance, 3-D, or on Grandma's refrigerator). Simply remember the rule—use the entire frame—and the photos will do justice to the work. Photographs have the added benefit of helping you record and document the process and effort that led to the finished piece.

Video has enormous possibilities for inclusion in portfolios. Performances as well as interviews with the child explaining the work are wonderful video applications.

A cautionary note: Unedited video can be deadly. It can put someone to sleep faster and more soundly than any uncle's travel slides. And, as the "medium is the message," the child will be judged by *your inability* to edit properly.

On the process: All of us want to be seen at our best. A child will resist the inclusion of "process" materials that are not polished. You must instill in the child a sense of respect for the effort as documented by these process materials.

RESPECT THE "CHILDLIKE QUALITY" OF THE CHILD'S IMAGE

THE INFAMOUS CHRISTMAS TREE NECKLACE

Just before the holidays, my five-year-old daughter came home from kindergarten sporting a "Christmas tree necklace." It was a perfectly formed plaster tree, four inches high, green on one side, white on the other, held by a red piece of yarn passed through a hole at the top. At first I was quite pleased; however, as I thought about it, I realized that she probably had very little to do with its creation. When I questioned her, she told me that her part was simply putting the string through the hole. She didn't even make the knot that tied it!

Though it looked very nice and pleasing to all the parents, the Christmas tree necklace represents a recurring problem with "children's work." In an effort to please parents, teachers often feel compelled to send home finished products that have involved little input from the child. Bottom line: The child is praised for something that she didn't produce, and she knows it. This devalues her and her work.

DOCUMENTS OF MEANING

PORTFOLIOS CONTAIN

DOCUMENTS OF **MEANING**.

EXAMINE WHY YOU OR

THE CHILD **CHOOSE** TO

INCLUDE OR **EXCLUDE**

CERTAIN THINGS.

THIS **CAN** BE

VERY **ENLIGHTENING**.

The Words

Any written pieces included in the portfolio should have a brief explanation, along with a date of course. Some people who see the portfolio, even the very interested (Gramps), may not have time to read each piece. Make the communication "user friendly." Include first drafts and other process materials for comparison.

Flexibility

The portfolio must be flexible. This is extremely important. All decisions made about either content or packaging must be open to revision. Why? The portfolio is a record of the person's accomplishments and who she is. It should be a record of constant learning, change.

Remember how deleterious prejudice is to the process of seeing? It is just as damaging to suggest to a young person that this is who she is, PERIOD. The concept of the portfolio is to encourage growth and change in that person.

Historical Perspective

Editing skills are essential. The portfolio should contain the best work that the child did at a particular time. The tricky part comes in encouraging a healthy respect for past work while adding new material that is obviously superior. It is essential for the child's proper development that she have a sense of where she's been, a comparative record of the improvements in quality that she has made. A healthy dose of history, past materials with dates, will give a greater appreciation of current successes and future possibilities.

HISTORICAL DOCUMENTS. *HUNTINGTON ROAD, 1986*

A SHARED TIME

The production of a good portfolio requires some discipline. Some materials will be obvious and you will naturally include them. But other deserving accomplishments will only make it into the portfolio if you are disciplined enough to put aside some "personal history" time at regular intervals. This should be a time of sharing between you and the child, recapping recent history and sharing any possible new portfolio inclusions. It is also important at these times to return to the portfolio to reexamine and enjoy the past work.

If you do this monthly, the child will develop with a strong sense of self. You will also share valuable personal time together. Lastly, a stellar family history will materialize. (And the child will be famous when the anthropologists come sniffing around a few thousand years from now!)

12

ANY QUESTIONS?

MONKEY SEE, MONKEY DO

I was traveling with my daughter, who was nearly two years old at the time. As we were returning to our hotel room one afternoon, she starting imploring, "Keys, Daddy, keys!" Naturally, I gave her the key to let her attempt to open the door. She started to put the key in the keyhole, stopped, put the key in her mouth, and then put it in the keyhole!

I wondered. Then I realized that nearly every time I approach my front door, I put a key from my key ring in my mouth, so that I can pick out the correct key using only one hand. The other arm is filled with her and her belongings. This made a big impression upon me. It is an example of how important observational skills are to human beings.

Summing it up: I recall the time a new parent asked me about child-rearing. My advice: "Monkey see, monkey do."

FOR FURTHER INFORMATION

The ending of this book is, of course, just the beginning. Sorry for being so trite, but it's true. I hope that working through the book has been an enjoyable process and a decent use of your valuable time.

Now the fun really begins. Using the principles and materials on which we have touched, you can increase your enjoyment and appreciation of life. Your heightened awareness may also lead you to recognize changes that you can help bring about to make this a better world for all of us.

I am ending this book with recommendations for books, films, and other resources that I have found to be rewarding and visually stimulating.

Books

The Art of Seeing by Aldous Huxley
Berkeley, California: Creative Arts Books, 1982
The great writer relates his personal experience attempting to ward off "certain blindness" at an early age. The book provides exercises Huxley used in an effort to improve his sight physically, while also creaking open the doors of perception.
Adults and teenagers

Envisioning Information by Edward Tufte
Cheshire, Connecticut: Graphics Press, 1990
A wonderful book on the various methods of communicating information visually. Informative charts and diagrams illustrate the author's "rules" for using visual information with integrity.
An adult book, also appropriate for teenagers

From Both Sides of the Desk: The Best Teacher I Never Had by Timothy Gangwer, illustrated by Donna Kiddie
Austin, Texas: Zena Books, 1990
A concise, often humorous treatment of the qualities that make a good teacher
All ages

Photographs by Annie Liebovitz
Milan, Italy: Amilcare Pizza, 1991
Very accessible, well-crafted images of celebrities; a great entree into a critical perspective of the icons of popular culture
All ages

Megaliths by Paul Caponigro
Boston: Little Brown, 1986
Exquisite black-and-white images with superb tonal values
All ages

Golf in the Kingdom by Michael Murphy
New York: Arkana, 1992
The essence of this strange game by one of the founders of the "metaphysical" Esalen Institute. All golfers should read this. None will.

Films and Television Programs

Quiz Show, a film directed by Robert Redford
Television and truth, never done better. Each shot meticulously framed. Some wonderful, albeit fleeting images of children and TV sets.
All ages

Do the Right Thing, a film directed by Spike Lee
Available on video
Lee's attention to detail throughout makes for a
stunning film. Notice especially the use of color;
the heat of the hot summer day can be felt by the
audience. The filmmaker transformed an entire city
block, setting the controlled frame for the
viewer's experience.
*Adults and teenagers; strong language throughout;
some nongratuitous violence*

Night on Earth, a film directed by Jim Jarmisch
Available on video
Simple premise: five taxicabs, five major cities,
the same night. A special concept of time and
imagery; touching, humorous, very offbeat—not
for everyone; some subtitles
Adults and mature teenagers

"Fawlty Towers," a PBS television series
starring John Cleese
Available on video
A comic exercise in timing and pacing,
mostly frantic
All ages

"CBS Sunday Morning"
A unique television show that values empty space
(quiet). Stories tend to be well-focused little
works of art.
All ages

"Power Plays," a PBS television series produced by
Andy Burnett and the Oxford Film Group.
Sports and the media. Look for the cutting-edge
framing used to demystify sports and celebrity.
All ages

"Sherlock Holmes Mystery," a PBS television series starring Jeremy Brett
A series based upon the deductive skills of Arthur Conan Doyle's super sleuth. This version presents a Holmes whose well-crafted character is not that of the normal hero. When my daughter was three years old, she said, "Daddy, I can't tell if he's good or bad." Well done.
Adults and teenagers; some nongratuitous violence

Software

Adobe Photoshop
Available from Adobe Systems
A powerful image-editing program; the creative possibilities are endless.
Any age with adult start-up help

Other Resources

Educational Workshops by Joan Goldsmith and Kenneth Cloke
2411 18th Street, Santa Monica, CA 90405
An extraordinary experience for teachers and administrators focusing on issues from maximizing classroom performance to administrative school change and labor issues. The future of education; these two gurus are dedicated and warm, if not downright hot.
Educators, K–12

JOAN GOLDSMITH CONDUCTING
HER RENOWNED WORKSHOP

KNOWING THE TRUTH

KNOWLEDGE IS

CONSENSUS,

WHAT WE CAN AGREE

ON [PRE-1492:

THE WORLD IS FLAT];

TRUTH IS ALL THE

POSSIBILITES.

Albert Einstein to

Marilyn Monroe in

Nicholas Roeg's film,

Insignificance

Impact II, The Teacher's Network
Ellen Dempsey, Director
285 W. Broadway, New York, NY 10013
A classic networking, nonprofit organization that brings together teachers and other educators in an effort to meet today's educational challenges. Constructive school change, innovative curriculum, and teacher empowerment are just some of the issues this national organization tackles head-on. *Educators, K–12*

REJOICING IN AMBIGUITY: TWO CHILDREN EXPERIENCE THE SAME SITUATION; ONE PERCEIVES IT AS TERRIFYING, THE OTHER AS JOYFUL.